Everyone is talking abou

I'm so phony sometimes that I can hardly ~~~
uncomfortable—very uncomfortable—for professional Christians like
me to read. But it is far more than an uncomfortable read—it is a book of
great hope and joy. John Stiles tells us the truth about the problem, but he
also points to the hope. With refreshing honesty and biblical insight, this
book could change your life and renew the church. If enough of us read
it, it could lead to another "Great Awakening." Read it, repent, and then
dance in the love and forgiveness of the God to whom this book points.

— **Dr. Steve Brown,** Host, Key Life syndicated radio program;
Author, *Three Free Sins: God Isn't Mad at You*

* * *

In my own childhood, hypocrisy in the church was the principle catalyst
that caused me to become an atheist for seven years. It was not until I
saw a genuine representation of Jesus in a Christian leader that my heart
was once again open to the claims of the Christian faith. Dr. Stiles' well-
researched and compelling book provides the perfect on-ramp for those
considering not merely the claims of Christians, but of Jesus Himself.

— **Francis Anfuso**, Senior Pastor, The Rock of Roseville, California;
Author, *Church Wounds*

* * *

When John Stiles says people are still watching us, he knows what he
is talking about. This is a book for all of us who publicly, in one way or
another, align with the Christian faith. Based on solid research, Dr. Stiles
reminds us that the Scriptures are more concerned with the way we treat
others and live authentically in a broken world than with making sure we
win battles or defeat our supposed enemies. I am going to be using this
book for a long time to come.

— **Chap Clark,** Ph.D., Associate Provost for Regional Campuses and
Strategic Projects; Professor of Youth, Family, and Culture, Fuller
Theological Seminary

"ALL THE DAMN CHRISTIANS"

A GLIMPSE INTO THE MIRROR OF HYPOCRISY

JOHN W. STILES, Ph.D.

SONFIRE MEDIA
A PUBLISHING COMPANY

For information contact:

> Sonfire Media, LLC
> 974 East Stuart Drive
> Suite D, PMB 232
> Galax, VA 24333

Cover & Interior book design by Larry W. Van Hoose

ISBN No. 978-0-9825773-9-4

MAY THIS PROJECT BE
BOTH A BLESSING AND A
CHALLENGE TO you —

"ONE HEART,
   ONE LIFE AT A TIME."

                    John Stiles

TO LIVE IS CHRIST!
                    Phil 1:21

Publisher's Notes

For purposes of simplicity, Dr. Stiles cited sources by means of parenthetical references with the source author's last name and the year in which the source material was published. Readers desiring to do further reading in the source text(s) will find full information in the References section at the back of this book.

Some anecdotes and supporting material have been obtained and edited, including changing some names, from various Internet sites. As much as possible, the author has made substantial good-faith effort to trace such material to their sources and to obtain written consent for use. Websites used are also listed in the References section.

Although the NIV does not capitalize pronouns for deity, Dr. Stiles has elected to do so in his text. Direct quotes from the NIV will use lower case for the pronouns.

Dedication

This manuscript is dedicated to Alvin and Mary Stiles, praying parents who trusted the Lord enough to allow me the freedom to always choose my own path (Proverbs 3:5-6). Thank you for your unconditional support and unwavering belief in my calling.

In the midst of this process, you have helped me learn, and to pass on to others, that our loftiest ambitions—the ones we most fear—are oftentimes the very ones we should pursue with passionate abandon. Your fifty-four years together have served as an innate stability in my every step, and as an inspiration toward which I aspire with the one God ultimately has for me.

I love and honor you, Mom and Dad.

"All the Damn Christians"

Acknowledgments

Much appreciation is expressed to my brother Michael—my "safety net"— who shaped and molded me as a writer by expertly editing most of my papers throughout my academic career, and who read every draft of this manuscript. He unselfishly treated this project with as much care and concern as did the author. Michael, you "hung the moon" for me long ago.

My deepest thanks and gratitude are extended to all of the following for your contributions to this book, whether reflected through the words on the page or through your words of encouragement and blessing etched on my heart: Francis Anfuso, Kevin Auman, Hampton Baxter, Steve Brown, John Bunn, Sharon Burcham, Chap Clark, Tom Gamble, Jack Gresham, Mazharul Haque, John Hobbs Sr., John Hobbs Jr., Ken Jenkins, Ken Koontz, Hunter Lambeth, Cort Langeland, Simon Park, Mac Powell, Chris Smeda, Eric and Sara Smith, Steve Taylor, Todd Terhune, Byron Vaught, Richard White, the late Gene Wiggins, Douglas Wilson, Randall Worley.

"All the Damn Christians"

Contents

"All the Damn Christians"

Introduction

The book you are holding began as an academic study. It ended as a journey.

But because of the inherent convictions and challenges, I have discovered that the journey has really just begun. This was a personal walk for me, a step-by-step process. I have struggled to walk every line, chapter by chapter. And in doing so, the unscripted conclusion wrote itself.

I have identified hypocrisy not as a collective problem of the church, but as an individual matter requiring self-examination, contemplation, and conviction on the part of everyone who calls himself or herself a Christian. Consequently, I have begun to walk this journey. And I can tell you this:

It ain't pretty.

However, this is the case in the midst of any journey toward freedom. And great are the rewards.

This book comes with some not-so-comforting news. Don't kid yourself: Hypocrisy is dark stuff. Still, there is much more good news than bad. To focus on the downside is pointless and futile. We showcase some provocative, attention-grabbing responses about Christianity from people in their own words. For example, the title of the book, *"All the Damn Christians,"* is a quote from a respondent. The survey responses presented throughout this book are a wake-up call to believers in Christ—a springboard to catapult us toward some kind of action and remedy. Without coming face-to-face with the root problem and offering a worthy solution, the book would not have been worthwhile to prepare.

My original research project examined attitudes and opinions about both Christians and the message of Christianity. This unique study considered the message-sending process of the Christian gospel. I asked people to write their honest reactions to and opinions about *Christianity, Christian people,* and *the gospel message.* The research instrument was a questionnaire (see Appendix A), and responses were handwritten. Each respondent could write as much or as little as he or she wanted, and—as you are about to see— opinions were thoughtful and impassioned.

Among the respondents, who were from different areas of the United States, the most frequently used term regarding their opinion toward Christianity and its followers was the word *hypocrisy* in various forms. For instance, one person wrote:

> *It [Christianity] conjures images of bigotry, hypocrisy, the moral majority, etc. Christianity is about unconditional love and acceptance. I don't see this.*

The research documented opinion through detailed descriptions of people's personal experiences, attitudes, and beliefs. Because I wanted to capture their true opinions in their own words, I took great care to avoid "leading" the respondents with my questions. Their candid responses served as the inspiration and the foundation for this book.

Perhaps because these questions are the type that we, the Christian church, don't particularly like to ask, the responses sometimes seem harsh. The findings are insightful, challenging, and even alarming. Nonetheless, they are informative, and I have provided a representative sampling of them in Appendix B. I encourage you to read and contemplate these responses as non-defensively as possible, for they compose a telling snapshot of how we believers are doing as we try to live and depict the good news of Jesus Christ among a post-Christian culture. Further to this end, I found it both helpful and necessary to expand my original research to include web-based material representing a wide range of stories and comments about Christianity. If we're wondering what people are saying, they're saying a lot— and we as believers can learn much if we are receptive and discerning.

Granted, it should come as no surprise that attitudes about Christianity and its followers are becoming more harsh. Long gone are the days when a teacher, television personality, or politician would be chastised for espousing views contrary to biblical teaching. That's just not the world we live in anymore. Whether heard via the media, from the lecterns of college professors, or through the responses of my study, the term *hypocrite* seems to be one of the most-favored words used to describe people of the Christian faith. And just as it did in the time of Jesus, the word carries a sting.

But is it possible that, whether from our zeal or our complacency—or perhaps from our failure to walk our talk—we Christians might bring some of society's negativity on ourselves? In other words, might the "style" (or lack thereof) in which we live out our faith actually be giving our detractors some valid ammunition?

Could it be that people are rejecting a story (the gospel) that is only half-told?

The most convicting finding of my study was that Christian people do not always communicate the gospel message according to the Scriptures. Thus, if non-Christian people are rejecting a message at all. in many cases they may be rejecting an inaccurate message.

So rather than present another "how to" formula for evangelism, I believe we need to take a trip back to square one and examine our position as individual believers from the standpoint of basic communication and genuine empathy.

Hypocrisy is not the main point of this book. It cannot be. Unfortunately, it has, does, and will exist. Instead, I've chosen to use these honest and alarming responses to help hold Christians more accountable in our daily lives as representatives of Christ, and to educate ourselves regarding secular culture. This is not to say that we should worry about what people say about us as a people group, but rather that we as the church should be very concerned if their viewpoints begin to affect the message of Christ.

Christ was many things—but He was always honest, always real, and He always represented the truth. The gospel of Christ was and still is clear, relevant, and life changing. May we all, as messengers heeding the Great Commission, endeavor to convey it as such.

Do we yearn to draw ourselves back into right relationship with the Lord, as Keith Green's lyrics so desperately depict?

My eyes are dry
My faith is old
My heart is hard
My prayers are cold
But I know how I ought to be
Alive to you, and dead to me.

If you care about your relationship with the Lord and with others enough to make these words your own personal prayer, then this book is for you. More specifically, the book is intended for you to be challenged and inspired to pass these words on to others.

"All the Damn Christians"

CHAPTER ONE

Beginning with the Man in the Mirror

Everybody thinks of changing humanity,
but nobody thinks of changing himself.
— *Leo Tolstoy*

The stage was set.

As the number of people swelled from hundreds to thousands, anticipation ran like an electric current through the hilly countryside. The overflow crowd left tread marks on their neighbors as they jockeyed for a better view.

Championship game? President of the United States? Rock concert?

No. Just a speaker. A guy all by himself.

No light show, no sound system, no drum roll ... not even a microphone. Just one man and his words.

Finally, the speaker emerges. He stands before them in a well-worn robe and dusty sandals. And they waited ...

But before He addresses the anxious crowd, Christ—as in Jesus Christ—is so concerned about one group among the thousands gathered there that He pulls His trusted ones around Him and warns them: "Be on your guard against the yeast of the Pharisees, which is hypocrisy" (Luke 12:1).

Though His message for the masses was burning inside Him, Christ took time to huddle with His confidants and tell them to be on the lookout for anything the Pharisees might be cooking up. *Something might be rising within them as they conspire against me,* He may have thought.

Was this paranoia or wisdom?

Do you think the title of this book might have ever crossed the mind of Jesus? Was this the line of thinking that evoked His righteous anger toward the moneychangers in the temple?

I would have a much higher regard for the religion itself if it weren't for all the damn Christians. Translation: *...if it weren't for all the hypocrites.* Has this thought ever crossed *your* mind, or have you ever uttered such a frustrated phrase?

If you're like me, you have.

Maybe you have experienced something similar to Ally's story.

Ally has been married for ten years. Most of those have been long, unhappy years as she has endured ongoing emotional abuse and physical abuse from her husband. Recently, when her husband's abuse was directed not only at her but also at Seth, her five-year-old son, Ally was forced to take action. Ally felt the only safe place to go for her, Seth, and her infant son Benjamin, was to a local women's shelter.

In order to conceal her new living location, Ally decided to cease contact with her husband's friends and associates while she initiated legal proceedings for a permanent restraining order and divorce. This included their pastor and their friends in the church.

Meanwhile, Ally's husband remained with the church, telling everyone that he couldn't imagine what had gotten into his wife. After all, he protested, the only thing that had ever happened in their entire marriage was that he'd accidentally "brushed her with his hand" one time.

As the day of the initial court hearing arrived, Ally looked forward to her attorney's presentation of the documented police reports of earlier incidents of domestic abuse. But to her astonishment, Ally saw familiar faces walk into the courtroom that day: six character witnesses, all mutual friends of the couple, all from their church, and all there to speak on behalf of her husband. All of the witnesses were men, and the key witness was their pastor.

Do you think Ally will ever be excited about returning to church?

Have religious people ever impeded your faith, witness, or ministry? After all, *religion* should not get in the way of *faith*. And religion certainly should not hinder the connection between a person and Christ.

But the sad truth is that there is nothing more annoying than a "religious" person. Think about it. If we strip all the stuff away, it's really just the *person* who annoys us, not necessarily the institution, or the morals, beliefs, and values for which that person stands. In other words, the problem is essentially how we represent our faith, not the belief system itself.

Pop icon Bob Dylan has endured years of analysis from Christians as to the authenticity of his professed faith in Christ. There has been an ongoing debate within Christian circles over whether Dylan is a "real" Christian, is "still" a Christian, "was" a Christian, or has "ever really been" a Christian. When asked about this controversy, Dylan's chaplain, two-time Academy Award winning songwriter Al Kasha, responded, "Bob loves Jesus. It's just the Christians that he can't stand."

Stepping Outside Our Circle

To step outside of evangelical Christian circles is to see a much different face of Christianity. And when we are willing to step outside our insulated circle, we most likely will see a serious problem facing us.

Hypocrisy.

No, hypocrisy is not the only topic of this book, but as far as we can deduce, it *is* a primary culprit when it comes to our witness to a hurting world.

Recent articles, research, and books have reminded us of this age-old cancer within the church. It may come as no great surprise to us, but when we hear it directly from our target audience, it does alarm us.

> *My husband and I stopped attending "church" because of this reason. We are still worshipers of God, still faithful, and try to be the type of Christians that God wants us to be. I think that when people are looking for a reason to believe or not to believe, they look at the examples that stand out the most. Faith is a confusing thing by its very nature, and when someone sees the bad examples, I suppose they figure "what's the point?"*

Does this bother us? It should.

A more significant question is *how should we respond*? Hopefully, we'll respond with a reformation of this epidemic, starting with the person in the mirror.

When I was fifteen, I attended a Christian camp whose camper age range was seven to seventeen. In those few weeks, I learned that true fellowship in the Lord's presence could impact one's entire life journey. As a college student, I became actively involved at these same camps as a counselor.

The summer camp that is most vivid to me as a counselor was themed "Show Us the Father," from John 14:8. We ministered to and prayed for so many kids who were from broken or abusive homes—many of whom were without a dad. Our role as counselors that week was simple: Love the kids, love them unconditionally, and show them the Father.

When this theme began to take root within the hearts of campers in the midst of the Holy Spirit's work, young and old alike began to glimpse the immeasurable love our heavenly Father so freely gives us. This was especially true in comparison to many earthly dads who, for various reasons, had been painfully deficient in displaying love and affection for their children.

Campers one after the other, broken and contrite, shared personal stories about their earthly fathers, testifying how the touch of the *heavenly* Father had restored their brokenness and self-worth during camp.

Eli said that he remembered only one thing about his father. His dad came home one day with two baseball gloves, a bat, and a ball. They went out to the backyard and started playing catch.

"After a while," Eli told us, "I had dropped the ball so many times that Daddy grabbed the two gloves, the bat, and the ball, took them in the house and laid them on top of the refrigerator, and never again played catch with me."

Taking the boy in his arms, our camp director, John Hobbs, said in his down-home eastern North Carolina drawl, "Let me tell you something, Eli—and I want the whole camp to hear this loud and clear. You have a heavenly Father who will not stop playing catch with you just because you drop the ball. He will be there for you, because His heart is to bring you back home to Himself as part of His family. And His love is ever extended to you. You can't dress up, look good, smell good, and act right *enough* for Him to love you one ounce more than He already does. And you can't mess up bad enough to make Him love you one ounce less. He just loves you. He just *loves* you."

Show us the Father.

The theme song used during that summer camp to help break, melt, restore, and heal so many hearts is the same theme and remedy I want to offer in this book:

Oh, Oh, show us the Father

For I want to hold His hand

The cry of my heart is to know the Father

For His grace by which I stand.

CHAPTER **TWO**

Who Is the Church?

*Don't stay away from church because
there are so many hypocrites.
There's always room for one more.*

— *Arthur R. Adams*

At age eleven, Donnie told his folks that he wanted to talk to the preacher about making a commitment to Jesus and joining the church. His mother was delighted to set up a special dinner before the Wednesday night service so the preacher and a visiting evangelist could come and seal the deal with Donnie.

At 5:30, dinner was hot and ready. So was Donnie. However, the special guests hadn't arrived yet. Then came 6:00 … and 6:30 … and the guests still had not shown up.

At the Wednesday night service, the pastor arrived a little late. He apologized to the congregation, mentioning that he'd even missed a dinner meeting beforehand. His reason for being late? There were several parties in front of the pastor and evangelist as they waited to finish the last hole on the golf course.

The meeting never happened … all because of a logjam on the eighteenth hole.

Donnie thought, *If this is what it's all about, what's the point?*

As to how Donnie's life was affected by this incident in the years afterward, we cannot be sure. Nor do we know if he ever made a commitment to Christ. What we do know is that, when Donnie was in his mid-thirties, he committed suicide. As we'll find out later, Donnie's death left a string of unanswered questions and a lingering restlessness in the hearts of those who knew him, including the pastor.

Are We Too Insular?

"The church is losing its saltiness. The church is in decay." In his signature baritone delivery, these are the words that thundered from the pulpit of my former pastor, now retired.

I remember thinking. *Preach it, Dr. Bunn. Go on; tell us how irrelevant the church is becoming in our world!*

I wanted to hear proclaimed everywhere these things I had researched and found so prevalent regarding the negative perceptions of Christianity and the church.

And I wanted to hear my pastor's magic remedy about how we can collectively control the wave of negativity and turn it around for God's kingdom on earth.

> *I'm not too sure because I'm from Ireland. What I have noticed about the Bible belief here is people say they are Christians, but really they aren't. They just go to church.*
>
> — *Study respondent*

We have this embedded mandate to be *in* the world but not *of* the world. However, we often run the risk of becoming too insulated in our Christian subculture, as if in a cocoon. Again, our example is Jesus, who did not seek insulation because He knew His protection and security would be provided by His heavenly Father. We are *in* the church in the sense that we are "covered" *by* the church, but we are not *of* the church either. We cannot and should not live there. If we are too heavenly minded we may be of no earthly good.

Do you catch the pensive complaint in the following comment?

> *I was an all-out supporter of church. I taught Sunday school for seven years and became an elder at my church. Very big accomplishment. I have taken lots of Bible classes, volunteered for church camp, and it all was wonderful until I couldn't take it anymore! I hated the mundane walking in, sitting, singing, and herding out of people. Insincere congregants who go to church believing that it will bring them closer to God, when it doesn't. I don't regret going—I always go at Christmas because I love to hear the story of Christ's birth again and again, but that's about it.*

We're fortunate to have an abundance of churches, which are our incubation chambers for worshipping God, learning His Word, and growing together in His love. Come fill up your cups, but remember that we also come together in order to *go out* and share our faith with others.

In this worship experience, the level to which we are *filled* directly corresponds to the extent that we are able to share. Evangelistically, *this* is why the church and corporate worship are so crucial. We are meant to be vessels carrying blessing. If we merely receive a portion or a sprinkling in our worship experience, how can we attempt to selflessly serve others?

On the other hand, if we go with open hearts, prepared to receive all that the Lord has for us, our cups will be filled to overflowing. It is this excess that flows so naturally off the top, so to speak—a reserve lavished upon us by God's Spirit in order that we may pour out the deluge onto others.

A missionary couple writes:

> *One thing we are thankful for is the education we have received— both secular and spiritual. The majority of people we work with in our health clinics in Guatemala are illiterate, and we see the impact it has on social status, earning power, and health. In addition, many of our Christian brothers and sisters in these churches don't have the luxury of reading God's Word for themselves or taking part in more in-depth study because of their limited skills. It is a blessing from God to have the opportunities we have as Americans, and we should use them in service to God.*

This is, in fact, the mandate for the church, the honor and privilege we have to affect others by sharing the free gift that has changed our lives.

Oftentimes the church is as portrayed in the words of this convicting song by the late Keith Green, "Asleep in the Light" ...

> *Do you see, do you see*
>
> *All the people sinking down*
>
> *Don't you care, don't you care*
>
> *Are you gonna let them drown*
>
>
> *How can you be so numb*
>
> *Not to care if they come*
>
> *You close your eyes*
>
> *And pretend the job's done*

'Oh bless me Lord, bless me Lord'

You know it's all I ever hear

No one aches, no one hurts

No one even sheds one tear

But He cries, He weeps, He bleeds

And He cares for your needs

And you just lay back

And keep soaking it in,

Oh, can't you see it's such a sin?

Cause He brings people to your door,

And you turn them away

As you smile and say,

'God bless you, be at peace'

And all heaven just weeps

Cause Jesus came to your door

You've left him out on the streets

Open up open up

And give yourself away

You see the need, you hear the cries

So how can you delay

God's calling and you're the one

But like Jonah you run

He's told you to speak

But you keep holding it in,

Oh can't you see it's such a sin?

The world is sleeping in the dark

That the church just can't fight

Cause it's asleep in the light

How can you be so dead

When you've been so well fed

Jesus rose from the grave

And you, you can't even get out of bed

As it turned out, my former pastor, Dr. Bunn, had no magic recipe for us to remedy the problem facing the church universal. Instead, he took the state of the church and personalized it by tossing it in our laps:

"If the church has lost its saltiness, if the church is in decay, then it is *we* who are losing our salt, and it is *we* who are in decay. For it is *we*, the people of God, who are the church."

CHAPTER **THREE**

Counterfeit Persona

I enjoy hearing them and then pointing out their
hypocrisy in practice.

— Study respondent, on
Christian message presentation

The question: What was the major obstacle to the ministry of Jesus here on earth?

It was the religious leaders of the day. "Beware," He warned, "the yeast of the Pharisees."

The yeast? Yeast *ferments*. What were the Pharisees fermenting?

Hypocrisy. Their own festering, legalistic, blind hypocrisy.

But what's behind hypocrisy anyway? If it's a disease, then how does one contract it?

Just after Jesus warned His disciples about the yeast of the Pharisees, He began to further admonish them by describing some of the pitfalls of hypocrisy. "There is nothing concealed that will not be disclosed, or hidden that will not be made known," He said. "What you have said in the dark will be heard in the daylight, and what you have whispered in the ear in the inner rooms will be proclaimed from the roofs" (Luke 12:2-3).

I didn't like it, because the message didn't feel like those people truly meant it. It seemed more like a performance.

— Study respondent

How ironic it is that strategically placed veils—meaning our good intentions and the masks we wear—are all colossal and *eternal* wastes of time?

Maybe, like the following young woman, you've wanted to remove your mask.

My whole life I had to live with a mask on. I made myself look like a "good girl." I would bring home good grades, and I never got in trouble in school. I knew what was right and what was wrong. But I got tired of pleasing everyone; I decided to make my own little private life. I began to drink. My parents never found out. For months, I got drunk every weekend. During this time, I met a friend who introduced me to witchcraft. I knew that witchcraft was bad, but just to have the chance to do something bad made me feel good.

Which Face Is the Real One?

Hypocrisy is derived from the Greek word *hupokrisis*, meaning, literally, "a reply." The word *hypocrite* came to denote a theatrical performer who speaks dialogue. It was used in reference to play-acting, role-playing, pretending—hence, acting insincerely. In everyday Greek language, hypocrisy meant to feign what one was not.

Playing a role.

It was the sense of play-acting, partially resultant from a Roman disdain for actors, that eventually brought about a negative connotation of the word. More precisely, society came to look upon hypocrisy as the assumption of a counterfeit persona.

This is closer to the New Testament meaning of the word *hypocrisy*. In New Testament times, an actor on stage did not merely play a role. Rather, he actually played two roles simultaneously by wearing one mask on his face and a different mask on the back of his head. This is how the expression "two-faced" originated. Accompanying the front-and-back masks was a similar front-and-back costume signifying two opposing roles.

This image kicks up the ante a few notches, doesn't it?

We all play roles. We perform them daily, and we all know the role of a Christian. We even have a guidebook for it. But obviously we haven't weighed the words of Jesus in Luke 12.

Ultimately, the charade is only for us. It accomplishes nothing positive and leads to confusion. When people look at us and see two faces, two costumes, it's natural that they'll wonder which face is the real one. Or whether either face is real. Which face does your own mirror reflect? Where is the authenticity, where Jesus and the abundant life reside? Consider the word *integrity*, which means the state of a person being whole, or one–not one person some of the time and a different person at other times.

> *I had been taught a lie—in church. I was told that I could be and should be perfect. I was far from perfect, so I pretended to be perfect until my hypocrisy destroyed my health and my family and nearly killed me. I did drugs and drank and cried myself to sleep at night. On a dark street in the city one night, I cried out, "God! Where are You? I can't find You! I hope I will before I die." Then through a series of small miracles God made that cry a reality—like the lost sheep in Luke 15, Jesus sought me until He found me.*

We are accustomed to the roles we play in everyday lives—at home, at work, in relationships. But we would never want to be accused of being a counterfeit spouse, parent, or employee. That's pretty grave stuff. After all, in our culture, role players (actors) are idolized but counterfeiters (criminals) are sent to the slammer. Your friendly superstore cashier has a handy highlighter to mark your bills on the spot for authenticity.

No one wants to be a counterfeit. Yet we have lowered the standard on what is acceptable in our own roles to the point that we have become imitators.

For too long we have stolen or borrowed another's face or actions in our relationships and responsibilities. We are responding to cues, signals, or symbols derived from some hodgepodge of media and society that has nothing to do with our core calling, the people we are, or the image of our Creator.

This is why we have become imitators.

Or, in the eyes of those who criticize Christianity: hypocrites.

In order to comprehend and begin to turn this tide, we must look not only at those who would scorn us, but also at ourselves. At ourselves as individuals. At ourselves as the church. In many ways, our detractors are right about us. In many ways, *we* are the problem. As despicable as it may sound to us, *we* are the Pharisees of our day.

We can continue to placate ourselves and gain zero ground. Or we can take action, one heart at a time, with each of us making a commitment: *I must personalize this problem. If I am unwilling to examine myself in this effort, I have not yet begun to fully personalize the gospel into my heart and life.*

Leo Tolstoy's quote that we are eager to change humanity, but not ourselves, was made over one hundred years ago, but perhaps rings even more true today.

Otherwise, really, what's the Christian life all about? Or as our Study respondents have implied, what's it all for?

> *I was like Saul of Tarsus—the chief of the Pharisees. I went to church every week, paid my tithes, and even went door knocking on weekends. However, no matter how much I did, I never felt "clean" inside. The problem was, I DID NOT HAVE JESUS IN MY HEART and was trying to work my way into heaven. Finally, I went to an old-time church where I heard the gospel preached with power. Hearing the TRUTH brought conviction to my heart. With tears in my eyes, I made my way to an altar of prayer, begging for salvation. The Lord gave me the assurance that I was looking for. I got up feeling "clean." I got something real that night.*

As you ponder such a commitment, envision with me this agent of accountability.

If there were a special highlighter pen that could gauge our authenticity as persons of integrity—that gave a true indication of our hearts for God—how often and where would we want to carry it? Would we be willing to take it with us into the dark, secret places? Into the inner rooms of our thoughts? Into the things we think, say, and do when no one is looking?

CHAPTER **FOUR**

The Greatest Story Ever Half-Told

The single greatest cause of atheism today is
Christians who acknowledge Jesus with their lips,
then walk out the door and deny Him by their lifestyle.
That is what an unbelieving world simply finds unbelievable.

— *Brennan Manning*

Lillian was a good, churchgoing girl.

It was the 1940s, the war was over, and America was an exciting place to live. Having been brought up in a very strict church, eleven-year-old Lillian was not allowed to dance. And as with any young girl, she was curious about anything she had not experienced.

One Saturday night, she and her friend Judy were running an errand when they stopped outside the community center where a dance was going on. Out of curiosity, they approached the window to get a peek at what had been forbidden. The people inside didn't look as bad as their upbringing had led them to believe. In fact, dancing looked like a lot of fun. After satisfying their curiosity, the girls made their way back home, thinking nothing of what they had done.

When Sunday morning came, Lillian went to church with her family. Everything was as usual until the preacher called out her name, and Judy's, and asked the girls to come to the front of the church. With a bit of nervousness and not a clue as to why they were being called to the front, the girls stepped forward.

Unbeknownst to the girls, another member of the congregation had seen them peering into the dance hall the night before and reported it to the preacher.

In front of their families, friends, and the entire congregation, the preacher verbally scolded them for what they had done. What a terrifying, horrific moment for a couple of preteens! They had simply peered into the window. They had neither entered the dance hall nor danced a step. Yet here they were, humiliated at the front of their church.

For the next seventy-four years, Lillian didn't darken the door of a church.

Many years later, a different pastor was making house visits in the neighborhood and knocked on Lillian's door. From within the house, Lillian, now eighty-five, called out, "Who's there?" The pastor introduced himself, only to be met with disdain from Lillian, who said that no pastor would ever be invited into her home.

After a bit of negotiating, the pastor was finally allowed to enter. As they talked, Lillian shared that the last time she had been in a church was that Sunday morning seventy-four years earlier. The pain and humiliation she had experienced on that morning were still as fresh to her as they had been on that distant day.

Broken Trust

At the core of hypocrisy lies betrayal and pain. Christianity offers hope—a path to life, forgiveness, and redemption. We tell nonbelievers that Christianity offers "life more abundant." So, people begin to believe it, at least enough to observe us more closely: they kick the tires and maybe even entertain preliminary thoughts of embracing our faith. Hope is dependent on trust. We ask nonbelievers to trust us because we live in Truth. So, with much caution, they timidly begin to trust.

And when trust is broken?

A heart breaks. Pain festers into bitterness. Bitterness spreads into different areas of our lives and clouds our vision. Unforgiven, bitterness can last a lifetime, robbing the betrayed of the incredible joy, purpose, and fulfillment Jesus so wants to give. Just ask Lillian.

The impact of hypocrisy comes from the hope that there is a higher calling, and that there is something greater to believe in. The belief that just maybe, all one may hope for could actually be demonstrated and embodied in this earthly life. And just when we begin to trust and believe that our longing may have found the real thing, reality hits and our hopes fall back to earth. We've been a fool to even believe.

We find this even with figures in politics, sports, or media. We feel let down, essentially betrayed, when we learn that our favorite figures take advantage of the position in which *we* seemingly have placed them. And how much more severe is the disappointment when it results from the behavior of those closest to us! So, in unpacking the cognitive process of hypocrisy, we must understand that it is a progression. Hope becomes trust, and trust becomes faith, and the failure of someone in whom we've placed our faith underscores our silly naiveté. Take away this longing for something truly good, true, and real, and there is no hypocrisy.

As a young girl, Lillian had foundational respect and trust in Christianity, but that trust was broken by a misguided, sanctimonious minister who publicly condemned her for a petty act of curiosity. Lillian had understood Christianity to be a faith of acceptance, grace, forgiveness, and love. But what she experienced, in humiliating fashion, was Pharisaical anger and judgment. In other words, hypocrisy. She had put her hope and trust in a message of love and grace, but its bearers tragically misrepresented God's message. A promising young spirit was trampled into cynicism toward the faith, and the result was a life spent miles away from the God Lillian had once loved.

A Sacred Trust

It is this progression of hypocrisy that we believers are challenged to interrupt. We must realize that the victim of hypocrisy is hope. This is our sacred trust: to affirm one's hope in Christ and to avoid doing that which would destroy it. And yet we've all heard stories like Lillian's, even in the Scriptures, and unfortunately we have authored some ourselves.

After one of my summer camp experiences as a high schooler, I returned home bold and ready to spread the love of Christ that I had so wonderfully experienced with my friends and counselors. I was relentless in my desire to share, and to the chagrin of my older brother, Michael, my zeal spread to his girlfriend, Rachel. She was an "it" girl—a great student and a fixture in all the popular circles. My family had made Rachel an item of prayer, so I suppose I thought it was my chance to usher her into the Jesus circle.

One day she called our house for Michael, but I, the hyper-impassioned Christian camper, answered. Rachel asked if I'd had fun at my summer camp. As I answered her question, I was overcome by emotion, and before I knew it I was sharing, then proclaiming, then crying and spewing—saying something to the effect of, "Oh Rachel, if you only knew how much Jesus loves you and wants to save you from going to hell …."

I blew it. I'm sure Rachel was scared, freaked out, or both.

It may be shocking to learn that Rachel did not rush to attend my camp the following summer. The Bible says, "How beautiful are the feet of those who spread the Good News," but I had shot myself in the foot. My feet weren't exactly "beautiful" when I tried to talk to Rachel that day. My overzealousness had caused me to misrepresent the most wonderful message in the world.

In general, we Christ followers probably could stand to add more zeal to our witness, but when we are unable to effectively balance it, to share the Good News in a respectful manner, the negative images stick with people like white on rice.

So at the core of hypocrisy lies pain—the anguish of disappointment, and the loss of hope. When hypocrisy rears its ugly head, the real hope that Christianity offers is often rejected—not because of the message, but because of the messengers.

> *I like your Christ, I do not like your Christians. Your Christians are so unlike your Christ.*
>
> — *Mahatma Gandhi*

Mispresentations and Misrepresentations

Sadly, if you were to speak to ten people today about God and spiritual things, it is likely that eight or nine of them would readily refer to some negative representation of Christianity—but say little or nothing about Christ Himself.

This became very evident in our study. In fact, when asked about the message of Christianity, a pattern surfaced in which respondents often used the misrepresentations as their scapegoat to essentially scrap Christianity altogether:

> *Like most religions, the foundations and practices sound good on paper, but the reality brings about much hypocrisy and downright lying, as well as judgmental beliefs toward others.*
>
> *I've just heard it too much. Leave me alone.*
>
> *What I like to boil it down to is the so-called Golden Rule, "Do unto others …." and be Christlike. But what is the message that we often see? That's why when people tell me that they are Christians, I often run.*

This pattern became so prevalent that two categories emerged to help explain the disconnect between Christian representation and the message itself: *mispresentations* and *misrepresentations*. These are distinctly different from one another, yet both do equal harm when it comes to our mandate to share the gospel in word, behavior, and deed.

People within the study who identified themselves as non-Christians who did not have a clear understanding of the gospel message responded in a manner that can be categorized in two ways.

First, the Christian message has been *poorly presented* to the respondents one or more times in the past. Examples of *mispresentation* include preachers who may distort the message, such as "hellfire and condemnation" types or financially driven televangelists; overzealous and/or offensive proselytizers who employ condescension or scare tactics in communicating the message; or short-term missionaries who may feel obligated to gain another salvation notch on their belts by using oversimplified, diminished commitment versions of the message. Among the responses underscoring mispresentation were these:

It was flashily done. It sickens me.

Basically, worship Jesus and give us money or you're going to hell.

I respond more to presentations that speak to me and not shout or browbeat me. Jesus didn't do this.

After a while, they are all the same and you become numb to the whole thought.

Second, the Christian message has been *wrongly represented* to the respondents one or more times in the past. Examples of *misrepresentation* may include public scandal or corruption within the established church; media stereotypes; professing Christians who come across as hypocritical with their attitudes or actions, and thus model the opposite standard; and Christian gospel pamphlets or tracts which may be viewed as offensive or judgmental. Responses that shed light on our tendency to misrepresent the gospel include:

I thought it was a bad idea to present it in a little booklet because people wonder what propaganda you're trying to spread.

I feel that it's overused and trite and is not a true representation.

I feel it's hypocritical because many people say they're Christian but in fact are not. (They don't live like it).

Incredulously, I was amazed at how he put down other faiths and the role of women.

Whether a direct presentation of the message or a representation of Christianity and its message, both of these share one resounding thread: human representation. The key word here is *human*, underscoring the fact that the proclamation of a perfect gospel message has been entrusted to imperfect human beings.

Just Point People to Jesus

Why can't we just point people to Jesus? It sounds simple enough, but this actually involves pointing others away from *ourselves*. As one of Jesus' disciples said, "Lord, show us the Father and that will be enough for us" (John 14:8).

Show us the Father. By pointing people to Jesus, we show them the Father, not ourselves. By introducing them to Jesus, we point them to the only one who introduces them to the heavenly Father.

So how do we show the Father to others by pointing them to Jesus?

I went back to some influential people in my life, people who pointed me to Jesus, and asked them how they modeled Jesus to me and to others. These are some wise folks who I know do it right. A good person to start with was my camp director and mentor, John Hobbs. John's the one who came up with the camp theme, "Show Us the Father." Here's how John answered my question.

> *My basic conviction is that you can't give what you ain't got! If you are planning to "show folks the Father," then you have to know the Father—His heart and His ways. Knowledge of both is essential. Jesus is the express image of the Father, and to know Jesus is to know the Father.*
>
> *If I press into intimacy with Jesus, then I will get to know my heavenly Father. And in getting to know my heavenly Father, I get to know*

myself. Knowing myself as my Father's Son frees me to love others without having to get their approval. If my identity is found in Him, then I am to live and love as He does, and my heart is always to live so that people get an accurate image of my Father.

This is exactly how Jesus pointed to the Father. He said, "The Father and I are one. If you have seen me, you have seen the Father. If you know me then you know the Father."

It is not my job to get people "saved"; it is my joy to introduce them to Jesus. I introduce them to Jesus by loving and living as He did! This means that people are not my projects, but we are all His projects. My joy is to love folks and introduce them to Jesus by having my Father's heart for them and by sharing that heart with them by the power of the Holy Spirit in whatever way He leads. Mainly it's by listening, loving as I've been loved, and wanting others to have the same dignity that Jesus wants them to have. I show people the Father best by having His heart and living like His Son.

A Story Half-Told

Scripture makes it clear that not every person will accept the gospel of Christ, and that it will be offensive to many. That's a given that we need to keep in mind as we wrestle with the more disturbing responses of our survey. This being said, we must be careful not to fall into a trap of assuming that all rejection or offense taken is due to this biblical acknowledgment of the human condition. Indeed, the study's results imply that many people who "reject" the message of Christianity have done so because the message has been mispresented or misrepresented by human beings. In fact, the evidence shows that they are rejecting a story (the gospel) that is only half-told. Are we, without realizing it, propagating a counterfeit gospel?

You can pick out what you agree with; everyone has their own opinion.

I do not know anything about the gospel.

Christianity does not = truth. I would reject the presentation because it is preaching Christianity. I am highly educated on the subject and already know that the gospel is not fact.

The Challenges We Face

As believers, we're faced with two challenges. First, Christians are challenged to be keenly aware of how significantly we may have convoluted the greatest news in the world, and to help rectify inaccurate representations of His message by simply pointing people away from ourselves to the person of Jesus Christ. What can happen when we do this?

Today, I'm in love with JESUS. All my life I was desperately searching for love. I experienced so much rejection that I could not talk to people. My loneliness brought me always to the wrong type of men. I was a prostitute and thought that God the Father was so angry with me, that He never would accept me. One day my little daughter pulled me to a church building. I looked to the cross and prayed: "Lord, if You really exist, please help us."

Then a woman came into my life and pointed me to Jesus. I felt a love and peace and asked her, "What is that?"

She said only, "This is Jesus. He is real!"

I was so touched at this name, and I'm still touched when I hear His name. I went home and I looked at my books to see if I could find more of Jesus. I found a Bible, which was laying there between all my terrible books. I never had a Bible, but it was there. I started to read in Isaiah 54:8: "In a surge of anger I hid my face from you for a moment, but with everlasting kindness I will have compassion on you."

In this moment, I felt the Lord was talking to me personally. He knew me. He knew how much I needed His salvation, His resolution…how much I needed Him. I fell on my knees and prayed. I invited Jesus into my life and I asked for forgiveness of my sins.

Every day I brought sins to Him, what I suddenly remembered, and I felt this wonderful peace coming. Oh, how I need Jesus!

He gave me back a joy, which I cannot say in words. Only sometimes the enemy wants to come back with memories, then I need to tell Him the truth from God's wonderful word: "I'm a new creation, no more in condemnation. Here in the grace of God I stand!"

The second challenge is for *non-Christians* to look to Jesus as the true representation of Christianity, not to imperfect humans who routinely disappoint others by mispresenting and misrepresenting Christ and His message.

I was raised in a church, and everyone thought that I was a Christian for years. But all the time, I was just playing a part and searching for something real in other places.

It wasn't easy. I looked at a few other belief systems and really didn't find what I was looking for. I guess all along I knew that what I really wanted was Jesus, but I didn't want to be a Christian, because I had been hurt by Christians.

When I was fourteen, my mom sent me to a Bible camp, and I reluctantly went. It was probably one of the best experiences of my life. There was something different in these Christians, and I wanted it. I accepted Christ into my life on July 1, 1991.

God wasted no time. He began to fill me with peace and hope, where before I had just felt hopeless and empty. And He began to use me to talk to other people who had felt the same way as I had before I came to God.

I just graduated from Bible College last week. God has been faithful and wonderful, and if He could change me from a hopeless searcher to a strong and fulfilled person, He can do the same for you.

So we Christians must first stop shooting ourselves in the foot. It's time to stop aiding and abetting non-believers' easy excuses for avoiding a Christian commitment because of our lackluster human modeling efforts.

Secondly, we must encourage non-believers to stop using our human failings, our mispresentations and misrepresentations, as easy scapegoats or smokescreens for their rejection of the faith...and to look to Jesus and His Word for the truth they seek.

The Ultimate Question

For the unbeliever, then, the ultimate question is not "What about all the hypocrites?" Instead, the ultimate question—with eternal consequences—is, "What will I do with Jesus?"

Consciously putting our faulty human representation aside, this must be the focal question for Lillian, for Donnie, and for all of us who have been hurt and disappointed by mispresentations and misrepresentations.

> *Let us fix our eyes on Jesus, the author and perfecter of our faith....*
> *(Hebrews 12:2)*

What will you do with Jesus?

CHAPTER FIVE

Stereotyping: The Echo Effect

Satan throws rocks over the wall of the church...
Christians then throw them at each other.

— *Anonymous*

Christians are so often accused of stereotyping or judging others that we are often stereotyped on this basis alone as collectively narrow-minded, bigoted, and judgmental. Are we branding ourselves?

> *Even though I'm a Christian, I've picked up negative stereotypes, especially that of religious right and super-conservative Christians as being extreme and rule-bound and close-minded.*

> — *Study respondent*

Due to being labeled this way, oftentimes it is not the message that is rejected as much as it is the *messenger* who is rejected. So where does stereotyping begin? Do we need to change the messenger, the message, or both?

All we can do is be better stewards of what we are called to do—what we are *commanded* to do: Tell others the good news of Jesus Christ. This is all we are responsible for.

Problem is, we are failing miserably. The Billy Graham Evangelistic Association says that approximately 98 percent of Christians never share the gospel personally!

I grew up in a Christian home, while attending church every Sunday for ten years. And not once was I taught about Jesus' salvation. When I was thirteen years old, I got caught up with drinking, stealing, smoking, lying, getting in trouble with the law, and boys. I was heading down the wrong direction, trying to fill the emptiness in my heart.

At that same time, my uncle was struck with cancer. The doctors gave him three months to live. He was the most influential man in my life and was very strong in his faith. I started questioning life. How could a man in so much pain and agony lift up his life to the Lord and glorify God? This changed everything.

On the day of his funeral, also the day of my birthday, I put forth all my sins and gave my life to Christ. Ever since, my life has never been the same. Every day I wake up with a sense of hope and completeness. I am now 17 years old, an honor roll student and very involved with the community. No more lying, cheating, and stealing, because I have the love of Christ. No matter where I go in life, I will always press onward and share the Word of God. No one deserves to be in that much pain. Philippians 4:13: I can do all things through Christ who strengthens me. Reach for the stars, tackle your dreams, with God by your side anything is possible. Life is temporary, God is forever. Where are you going in life? Are you heading down the right direction?

Most of us clearly are not telling others about Jesus on a regular basis, either because it isn't a priority or because it just doesn't occur to us. In fact, the Barna Group reports that only 35 percent of Christian adults feel a responsibility to verbally share their faith with others. The real danger here is that our silence itself can lead to mispresentations and misrepresentations because we routinely allow others to tell our story *for* us. And while some may tell it well, far too many tell it poorly—by either the lives they lead or the words they utter.

Either way, by either our silence or our misguided methodology, we are shooting ourselves in the collective foot, wrecking our platform.

Some refer to it as "Christian cannibalism."

> *They are lazy about standing up for their beliefs, or they are pushy.*
> *They do not work together effectively. They tend to be more worldly*
> *than spiritual and therefore do not make a convincing testimony.*

> — *Study respondent*

Our mispresentations and misrepresentations lead to negative stereotypes. Then, with every real or perceived additional mispresentation and misrepresentation, the stereotype is further fueled, perpetuating an endless cycle we call the *echo effect*. In other words, an endless circle.

Where and when does the stereotyping *end*?

Why Are Christians Stereotyped?

Approximately eighty million Americans profess a belief in Christ. This is a significant percentage of our country's population. Then why does it seem that Christians are constantly getting picked on by the press, by government officials and private interest groups, and by seemingly anyone who has a microphone? And why is it that Christians seem not to fight back? Is it because we're taught to turn the other cheek? Doubtful, since it is reported that *less than 5 percent of those eighty million profess a biblical worldview.*

Christian pollster George Barna defines a biblical worldview as the belief that absolute truth exists, that such truth is defined by the Bible, and that the believer adheres to six specific religious views—including the belief that Jesus Christ lived a sinless life, that Satan is real, and that the Bible is accurate in all its teachings.

But in what might be the biggest disconnect in the history of Christianity, this basic, biblical worldview is rejected by more than 95 percent of those eighty million who profess a belief in Christ.

Honestly, how can this be?

For centuries, Christians have looked upon the Bible as the ultimate guidebook—the inspired Word of God. Jesus, in whom we all profess to believe, affirmed God's Word and its essential precepts of true faith in Him. So how is it that seventy-six million people who identify themselves as Christians do not subscribe to a worldview set forth by the Word of God? Could it be that the power of stereotyping is so strong that we do not wish to be categorized, and thus ostracized, by society? How many times have we heard Christians say, "Oh, but I'm not one of *those* Christians." Hold on a second. Which Christians are *those* Christians? The ones who believe in the historicity and reliability of the Bible? C'mon somebody, say it ain't so!

> *I want to talk about the Christian stereotype. The one where Christians are seen as God-fearing, holier-than-thou, self-righteous, preachy, pompous do-gooders, and most importantly, hypocrites. I know the stereotype well—I used to think a lot like that myself. My experiences with "Christians" only enforced my perception of that stereotype. It's one of the reasons I did not speak openly about my faith once I decided to embark on a spiritual quest. I didn't want to be considered one of "those people."*

The point is that we act as though we are in the vast minority, when in actuality this is not the case at all. But the power of stereotyping and its resultant peer pressures has seemingly stifled us at every turn. Why does this seem to be a perpetual cycle? Are Christians being pushed into a corner by the proverbial bully on the block—that is, a cynical, scornful society and media? Why, then, is stereotyping so pervasive and powerful?

I believe, with the help of media and stereotypes, that I've been influenced [into] thinking all Baptists condemn people to hell and the Islam religion is a truly evil religion.

— *Study respondent*

I often feel annoyed with the Christian community for the hypocrisy displayed most prominently in the media. I also feel that the media is unfair in its representation, almost as if they go out of their way to find the poor examples and stereotypes of a group.

— *Study respondent*

Did you detect a shade of empathy in this last statement? Empathy is a good start to unlocking the mystery behind the mental processes of stereotyping. Empathy should be an innate by-product of any Christian person—someone who senses, cares about, and is open to the feelings of others. But this does not always come naturally to us as human beings. Sometimes it's hard. But if we can begin to understand what goes on in the head of another person, then we are certainly on our way to better understanding what makes a person tick. Oftentimes what one thinks and feels essentially dictates how the individual views oneself, views others, and makes sense of his or her world.

Lest we feel that "getting into the head" of someone would lead to manipulation or zealous coercion, the truth is that the opposite is true. Genuine empathy can lead toward a much deeper awareness of an individual through a more thoughtful and sincere effort to know and understand, not to lecture and convert.

So in order to comprehend, combat, and overcome the echo effect, it is important to identify and empathize with some of the common mental patterns that go into stereotyping. Otherwise, we may never interrupt—and reverse—the cycle.

Unpacking Stereotypes

Stereotypes rely and feed upon overgeneralizations. Overgeneralizations reflect a perception that all members of a given group have the same characteristics and traits (Oskamp, 1991). To a certain degree, stereotypes play a useful—and probably unavoidable—part in everyday thought. However, they may become dangerous when they blur or prevent an adequate understanding of a more complex reality. In and of themselves, stereotypes could be considered contradictory, if not hypocritical in nature. Consider, for instance, that stereotypes are often used to describe groups or classes of people with whom the stereotyper actually desires to be identified; at the same time, stereotypes are also used to describe other groups or labels from which they wish to distance themselves.

Let's face it, we are bombarded from all sides, so we cannot define and make sense of each portion of the overabundance of stimuli we receive. On the positive side, stereotypes serve a practical purpose to essentially help sift and categorize the complexities of our society. More negatively, they allow individuals to guard their conscience by rationalizing prejudice against a person, group, or class (Allport, 1954; LaViolette & Silvert, 1951; Saenger, 1953).

> *It's hard not to stereotype, isn't it? Depending on your background, experiences, influences, etc., at some point in your life you'll make a statement or do something that stereotypes another person or group. In the right context, stereotypes can be funny. The best comedians make the audience see themselves in such stereotypes.*

In everyday life, stereotyping allows us to avoid confronting the complexities and contradictions in our own attitudes or experience. When faced with something we do not wish to deal with, stereotypes ostensibly help us push the issue aside, allowing us to sort things into tidy categories in our thinking. This is precisely why stereotyping is often alluded to as a device of the simple-minded—those who will not allow themselves to really think. Perhaps this is why Christians are so often accused of stereotyping others. As if using a crutch, we can default to these mental processes and simply move on, getting back to a higher priority within our personal agendas.

However, stereotyping goes both ways. Everyone does it, often unconsciously. And if ever there were a group or class of people who have been stereotyped, it is those who embrace the Christian faith. When asked for their opinion of Christian people, respondents said:

> *Insecure, dependent on the idea of a guiding force as the only reason why things happen. They accept events without questioning or looking too much into it. Also, judgmental, often to the point where they condemn and are hypocritical.*

> *I think the media has given me the impression that most Christians are undereducated people from small rural towns in Middle America, or rich conservative bigoted white men, or people who aren't flexible in their opinions and want to convert you, too.*

For a multitude of reasons, not every person desires to know every Christian, or for that matter, could ever meet every Christian. So it becomes easier to simply categorize all Christians as one.

> *Media images of Bible-thumping Christians are far from the day-to-day Christians I know. Focusing so much on extremists leaves the viewer with a bad taste in their mouth when they say the word "Christian."*

> *— Study respondent*

> White Christian people are shown to be very religious, law-abiding citizens [who] go to church every Sunday and pray before dinner.
>
> — *Study respondent*

It is clear that some stereotypes of Christian people are based solely on the fact that, as Christians, we ourselves are guilty of stereotyping others. Shades of the echo effect.

Exemplifying this avoidance of truth, one person responded to the question about Christian people by saying, *Yikes! Good and bad, I personally stay away from finding out if a person is of any religious affiliation.*

Birth of a Stereotype

Such categorical avoidance protects us from having to think more deeply, from regarding individuals as individuals and giving them the benefit of the doubt. The origins of stereotypes seem clear. Once people are exposed to stereotypes, whether through the media or through social interaction, the representations exist in the memory as mental associations, oftentimes perpetuating an *indelible link* (Nisbett & Ross, 1980). As one respondent describes, it's an image that can be tough to shake:

> Media play a role in sending images—stereotypes that are or become part of popular culture. They send us narrow conceptions about, say, gender or masculinity. In the same way, images and manners of depicting Catholics convey a message that Catholicism is a cult of child molesters.

As illustrated in the chart on page 40, "Climates of Threat in Christian Message Communication," once a stereotype is embedded in our minds we no longer have to entertain the notion; our guard is up, our ears are turned off, and our minds are closed.

The most important function of our quick assignment of persons to a social category is to simplify and systemize (Tajfel, 1981). Though it seems as impersonal as shuffling cards in a deck, we all do it. It occurs within us immediately and automatically and it takes only a moment's time. The categorization of individuals into a social group is a common mental process of learning and adapting, and serves to help people make sense of the world around them. For example, when asked one's opinion about the religion of Christianity, one person responded:

Mind control, frightening, oppressive, anti-feminist, and hateful.

Strong words, indeed. They make one wonder who this respondent personally knows in Christian circles who caused him or her to form such a categorization. Our next thought might be that it's not us, so we must be okay. Hostile opinions about Christianity like the one above tend to follow a common course, depicting an almost instantaneous progression from disagreement to outright rejection of the gospel message.

The crucial question here is, do negative stereotypes directed toward Christianity and its message seem to be increasing as indelible links in the collective mind of society?

CLIMATES OF THREAT IN
CHRISTIAN MESSAGE COMMUNICATION

MESSAGE CONTACT

Through a selected medium, personal approach,
or the random mention of the message through
unselected/undesired medium.

DISSONANCE

Disagreement with or contradiction of the message.

Former images, mispresentations, misrepresentations,
and categorizations.

INHERENT STEREOTYPES

Allow individual to avoid complexities and contradictions
in one's own experience.

TRIGGERING OF DEFENSIVE COMMUNICATION TACTICS

Deliberate misrepresenting or misunderstanding by
the recipient of the sender's motives.

The Trigger and the Link

Do non-Christians have a sort of built-in "Christian People Radar"? Why do many nonbelievers almost instinctively react defensively at even the slightest reference to Christianity?

In a word: *stereotyping.*

Ironically, while Christians are so often accused of stereotyping others, the nonbeliever just as readily stereotypes the Christian faith and those who espouse it. It's another result of the echo effect.

To naturally and comfortably address spiritual things with someone, demeanor and context can make all the difference. But we cannot always dictate a context conducive to addressing spiritual issues, and we certainly cannot control another person's reaction when we talk about what we believe. Consider a context in which you or I might make a low-key mention of God, or perhaps comment on the beauty of creation. Unfortunately, so many people believe they've had such a negative experience with some form or faction of Christianity that even the most benign mention of the faith may set off a screeching alarm in the hearer's mind. At this point, *dissonance* has occurred— disagreement with the message before even hearing it.

It's a result of inherent stereotypes.

That alarm immediately evokes negative memories of encounters, images, conceptions, mispresentations, misrepresentations, and categorizations from days past. The negative memories stir up negative emotions, and when emotions are stirred, the indelible link is formed.

Our general question about one's opinion of the religion of Christianity prompted one respondent to readily mimic the mantras and rants catalogued in his mind:

> *Stereotypes—"Bible-banging Baptist"—God keeps "laying things on their hearts" to do stuff until they do something stupid [or] wrong, then it's "the devil, the devil did it!"*

This link is almost visceral. The alarm sounds and the hearer's heartbeat quickens as he feels a climate of threat. It's natural to begin looking for an expedient route of escape. And until the hearer can break free—especially if he feels the communicator is intent on winning control or exerting superiority over him—he will likely trigger and deploy defensive tactics.

> *I tried Christianity because it seemed like the good thing to do, to make a long story short. I instantly became horribly depressed hearing the news that my family and friends and most of the world would be doomed for eternal torture if they weren't "Jesus freaks," for lack of a better word. This went on for a good two years and I was in mental hell because it all seemed so real...*

When a hearer feels cornered, he immediately links what he's hearing and feeling to a past negative experience or perception. Making this link elevates the hearer's emotional response, kicking in the various defense mechanisms he's installed over time to protect himself from such offenses. Defensive communication can present itself in a number of ways: an argument, a retreat, a shrug, a shout, a hand, maybe even a finger. In short, the blow-off.

Translation: *Don't go there with me.*

The "Climates of Threat" chart displays the cyclical nature of stereotyping and how it progressively leads to defensive reactions from the recipient. Not exactly a theory of rocket science, defensive communication basically occurs when people hear what they do not wish to hear. In other words, people may automatically react defensively about Christianity and its messages because of inherent stereotypes that are already embedded within their psyche from either past experiences or from hearing others express their own negative stereotypes. When a message contradicts a recipient's values and assumptions, the reaction can range from not concentrating on the message to deliberately misrepresenting or misunderstanding the motives of the sender as well as the message itself.

It becomes easy to understand why many of the responses to our study seem combative, sometimes even vindictive, toward the messenger. In most cases the recipient is recollecting a prior experience. While the current messenger may not be particularly offensive or forward, he or she may take the cumulative heat that has built up within the recipient from past encounters, perceived wrongs, or exposure to negative stereotypes. Responses documented in this study reveal that stereotypes and misconceptions of Christianity and its followers are a legitimate and powerful deterrent of the very message Christians are supposed to represent. As one respondent said,

> *I generally dislike monotheistic religions—they're too bossy, unquestioning, and conforming.*

Most Christians are aware that many people have strong opinions such as this. So to avoid being painted by such broad strokes, many of us avoid the categorization by becoming somewhat chameleon-like, blending into the mainstream and making as few waves as possible. At the same time, some of us exist quite happily in the insulated comfort zone of our Christian subculture. In those rare times when we venture outside of our comfort zones, we feel like fish out of water. We'd rather jump back into the downward flow than fight the upstream battle.

Is There an Antidote?

We really have no idea at what point this progression of disagreement begins. In other words, when and why do the negative responders' inner alarms sound?

It might have been the word *Christian* in the question.

It might have been the way the person asked it.

It might have been the body language of the person who asked it.

It might have been something from another source or stimulus.

It might have been some repressed anxiety, anger, or bitterness.

Or, it might have simply been a greasy lunch that triggered the defensive reaction.

We just don't know. And we won't know until we get into the heads of others.

But we can't get into their heads without getting into their hearts. And neither happens if we do not sincerely care for the individual through listening, loving, and empathizing. Most importantly, our efforts are useless in and of our humanistic selves if the Spirit of God is not going before us. Consider Jennifer's story:

> I had an abortion at age nineteen and I was supposed to be a Christian. I felt as if Jesus would never forgive me because I had already accepted Him as Lord and fallen away. All kinds of guilty feelings flooded my mind. There was always this empty feeling from the abortion. But one day I told Jesus He could have my pain. I

couldn't take it anymore. Without the power of His Holy Spirit, I knew I couldn't make it because I wasn't strong enough. I encourage you to lean on Jesus because He will forgive you and heal you ... Matthew 11:29-30 says, 'Take my yoke upon you and learn from me, for I am gentle and humble in heart, and you will find rest for your souls. For my yoke is easy and my burden light.'

This is the lone antidote to stereotyping. Because of God's Holy Spirit within us, we can know when and where it ends.

It ends with the church.

And who is the church? We are. You and I. It's not some ethereal institution, council, or pope. We the people are the church, and by the Holy Spirit we have the grace and the power to end hypocrisy and stereotyping.

One individual at a time.

Like racism, hypocrisy and sin are passed down, generation to generation, family to family.

Culturally embedded. Ingrained. Repressed.

But it is not innate to our nature.

When will the echo effect end? Do you believe it can end?

Are hypocrisy and stereotyping somehow larger than God?

CHAPTER **SIX**

Unmasking Hypocrisy

"Let he who is without sin cast the first stone."
— Jesus Christ (John 8:7)

So...

We can't pin the blame on the church.

We can't pin it on the preacher.

We can't pin it on other Christians.

We can't pin it on stereotypes.

On whom can we cast the blame for the culturally embedded perception of Christian hypocrisy?

The man in the mirror.

If we, as representatives of Christ, are to begin to overcome all the negative imagery and perceptions of hypocrisy, we absolutely must begin to accept the blame ourselves—as individual Christians.

Each of us has inadvertently mispresented or misrepresented the message, heaping more fuel on the fire. Individually, we are hurting the team. It is our responsibility to emerge from the hidden, secret places—from the abyss of hypocrisy—and climb out into the light with a true, refreshing representation of dynamic Christian faith.

First we must personalize and accept our part of the problem, as Valerie did:

> *I felt like I was the lowest, dirtiest thing on earth. I didn't think Jesus could forgive me for all the sin I had wallowed in. I had been raised by strict parents; but once I left home, I drank, partied, and even ended up cheating on my husband. Time and again, I would go to church, claim to come back to God, then allow the lure of worldly lusts to pull me away from Christ. About three years ago I started going to church again, and Jesus touched my life. I turned back to God.*
>
> *He showed me that when I repented, asked Christ to forgive me, He forgave me! My life has not been the same since. God's Word actually has changed me! The way of life I was living changed for me and my family. My husband started commenting on how changed I was.*
>
> *"Now you are clean by the Word which I (Jesus) have spoken unto you." His Word is truly a life changer.*
>
> *I stopped looking back and started looking forward to Christ. Oh, life has its trials and tribulations, but I have learned that this is a part of life. The difference is that Christ is with me every step of the way. I hold to Hebrews 13:5: "I will never leave you nor forsake you." That is truly a comfort, as well as James 1:2: "Count it all joy, when you fall into various trials." I have learned that these trials only come to make me stronger, closer to Christ, and [they get] rid of some way or habit that was not like Christ. God is truly good, and I am so glad to have the knowledge that He loves me.*

The key that unlocks the remedy to hypocrisy is that we stand up to our own will and examine our private lives, thoughts, and tendencies. If we can muster up the courage to be honest with ourselves, we can begin to curb society's negative perception of Christianity in order to advance the kingdom of God here on earth.

And how do we do that, exactly?

Personal, Private Molehills

For far too long we have looked at the hypocrisy of the church as a collective problem that can't be tackled.

This is a lie. It's not some ethereal collective mountain of hypocrisy we face.

Rather, it is a juicy assortment of personal, private, individual molehills that we are unwilling to surrender to the Lord.

We can, indeed, stop the bleeding, if we remove the mask behind which we so often hide.

To her credit, Valerie looked this notion square in the eye. Countless others, including myself, have also wrestled with molehills. In fact, genuinely searching our own hearts is an enormous struggle that we would frankly rather not endure. But examine ourselves honestly we must, for our hesitancy to do so is why we do not heed the command of our Lord to tell others about Him. With lives unexamined, we naturally do not feel worthy to represent Him.

> *I will be the first to admit that I am far from perfect, and while I aspire to be a better Christian, I make mistakes (and sin) all the time. That's right, I sin. I am a sinner. During this journey of faith, I have come to accept that fact. What I don't do is hide behind my faith, or use it as an excuse for my behavior. Honestly, I'm still learning, still wrestling with what I've learned, still trying not to sweat the small stuff. Yes, I have done stupid, STUPID things.*
>
> *I think part of being a Christian is the drive to be better, not just in what we do or say, but in every aspect. Some days I do better than others.*

Imperfect Representation of a Perfect Message

Hey, it beats me why almighty God chose *us*—human beings who sin, fall, fail, burp, scratch, and sneeze—to represent the greatest message in the history of mankind. As one of my seminary professors said, "At one time God spoke through an ass, and He's been doing it ever since."

Right, so I am God's agent. Sounds like a bad idea for a movie script. The mission is far beyond me, and it seems like I may never measure up. But maybe that's the point...

The power is in the message itself, not in the messenger. "The Father loves the son and has placed everything in his hands" (John 3:35). Maybe we should just get over ourselves and trust the message, I mean, considering its author and all. The *message*—it's the same message that penetrated the pain of Jennifer, that cleansed Valerie from within, and that once touched you. It's the message you trusted and that changed and rearranged your whole being!

Like a teenager in front of the mirror on prom night, we are so preoccupied with ourselves that the focus begins and ends with *us*. But the fact is, it's not just about us. And the message does not *belong* to us. It is God's, and for some inexplicable reason He has appointed us—you and me—to share His good news with the world.

But while entrusted with this incredible message, we tend to be concerned or preoccupied about our *lack* of something. We feel we don't have sufficient intellectual knowledge, biblical knowledge, speaking ability, coolness, and so on.

Smokescreens, really. These are all mere smokescreens for the fact that we don't want to be rejected. Which is why it's easier to go on a foreign mission trip and share with others we will certainly never see again than to knock on doors in our own neighborhoods. This way we fulfill our quota and can feel good about ourselves and our service.

We know that many will reject the gospel. Scripture is quite clear on that.

And we will always be called hypocrites. This moniker has been stamped on us from the very foundation of the church, since the origin of Christianity, since a place called Eden. We will always be called hypocrites simply because, unlike our pluralistic and universalistic society, we subscribe to a standard. We have absolutes, not just ideals and ideology. As one respondent wrote:

> To say that Christians are all good, or are all hypocritical, is a stereotype that is entirely false, but is claimed every day as an excuse to ignore Christianity.

Increasingly, it seems, people are trying so hard to believe in everything that they actually believe in nothing. Consider Dillon's journey:

> I know there is some sort of God. I can't make the logical leap necessary to believe everything came from nothing. Nor can I believe that the design we find in the universe is the result of random chance. But I don't think that God is interested in communicating with us, or He would have done so in a non-ambiguous manner [so] that we don't have to rely on merely the word of other humans or questionable "supernatural" experiences to verify. I waver between the idea that He has a fore-ordained plan set out, which I can only hope will be to the good of all (something I hope but have no evidence for) and the idea that God is just an impersonal observer, and we're all just His mad experiment. So I guess you could say I'm agnostic between deism and theism.

Dillon's response characterizes an inordinate number of young adults who were raised in the church yet find themselves in a disillusioned search to fill a remaining void. We all know about it: There is a growing contingent in the world—among them some regular churchgoers and even some who profess belief in God—who live by no absolutes, no moral code, believing in nothing except what they can see and touch.

Can you imagine going through life being so tolerant of everything and everyone that you stand for nothing—except against those who stand for something?

Can you imagine subscribing to no moral code or standard and then turning around and ascribing hypocrisy to those who do?

Welcome to the world of reverse hypocrisy.

As Martin Luther King, Jr. once observed, "A man who doesn't stand for something will fall for everything." What society does this statement bring to mind? The one outside your window, perhaps?

A Mild Case of Christianity

Some feel that hypocrisy, whether actual or perceived, is so prevalent because of the many nominal Christians among us. Do you know what the definition of *nominal* is? "Not real or actual; hardly worth the name."

Convicting, to say the least.

The world is accusing us of being casual or nominal Christians who have a mild case of Christianity, but not a faith that is real or actual. To their thinking, as they regard us, the term Christian is "hardly worth the name."

Is this the type of Christian life you are leading? Is it the kind of Christian life you want to live?

How would you define yourself as a Christian, as a representative of Christ?

How would others define you?

Are you truly being changed, inside and out, by the faith you profess— by the Spirit of God who came to reside within you when you gave your life to Him? Are you listening to His guidance, living a life that honors Him and is true to His Word? Are you allowing His Spirit to make you more and more like God's Son, Jesus Christ, every day?

Regardless of whether the world's view of believers is built on negative personal experience, misperception, or stereotyping...or even if it's built upon the sad truth that we sometimes drop the ball badly as representatives of our Lord...the challenge is clear for all of us. It's time to shed the old and make a conscious decision to bring in the new.

> *It is never too late to be what you might have been.* –George Elliott

As Christians in touch with the power and guidance of God Himself, we can achieve this. We must. The apostle Paul underscores the importance and the benefit of such a mind-shift:

> *Do not conform to the pattern of this world, but be transformed by the renewing of your mind. Then you will be able to test and approve what God's will is—his good, pleasing and perfect will.*
>
> — *Romans 12:2*

If we are to be called hypocrites (and we always will, by someone) then let it be for the *right* standard. Let it be for the right attitude and the right voice. Let it be because we are actually trying to live holy lives in mind, soul, body, and spirit, as we are called to. Then, by all means, let them call us hypocrites as much as they want.

Why?

Because we have a standard like no other. His name is Jesus.

Our job is to point people to Him and away from ourselves.

Do not let it be that people reject a counterfeit gospel *mispresented* by another because we *misrepresented* it by biting our tongue.

The late Adrian Rogers, revered pastor, speaker, author, and Bible teacher, put it this way:

> *Don't let counterfeit Christians keep you out of heaven. Now, why would I make such a strong statement? Because you could let them if you believe the stories their lives are telling. Let me set you straight. A counterfeit Christian is actually a backward testimony of God's Truth. You see, people don't counterfeit gum wrappers. They counterfeit $50 bills, $100 bills. Why? Because a $100 bill is worth something. And every counterfeit Christian that you see is a testimony to the real worth of being a true Christian.*
>
> *And another thing—don't ever let a person use [the term] hypocrite as an argument against Christianity. Every now and then somebody tells me, "Oh, there are some hypocrites in your church." I say, "Do tell!" A hypocrite is not an argument against Christianity; a hypocrite is a wonderful argument in favor of Christianity. Remember, one of the twelve apostles was a hypocrite. Counterfeit Christians and hypocrites don't prove what we believe not to be true; they are proof [that] what we believe is true.*

Counterfeit Christianity is our hypocrisy. It is our sin. And after years of thought, study, research, and introspection, I don't see a bit of difference between the two.

At its root, hypocrisy is sin. It's not some newfangled term or nuanced, euphemized marketing package. It's just sin. We haven't cut it down to size to give us a fighting chance. Really, at the core of it all, can we view hypocrisy as anything other than sin?

Who among us is without it?

Helpful hint: "In the event of an emergency, place the oxygen mask over your own mouth first. Then take care of those around you."

We must take care of our own sin first. Ask God to reveal and cleanse you of any hypocrisy or hesitancy that may be misrepresenting Him to those around you. Commit to living authentically, as He wants you to live, guided and empowered by His Spirit within you. Then, without going bonkers, breathing normally and naturally by the Spirit within you, assist those around you. Let them see God's love, joy, peace, patience kindness, goodness, faithfulness, gentleness, and self-control in your words, attitude, and actions. (See Galatians 5:22-23).

No Standard = No Hypocrisy

I have not selected a religion or particular belief because I do not want to say I am a Christian or another religion and contradict my beliefs with my actions.

— *Study respondent*

You see, in this sense, compared to the world we *are* hypocrites—because we are called to and we attempt to live our lives after the "author and perfecter of our faith," Jesus Christ (Hebrews 12:2). In the original Greek, *perfecter* is defined as "originator, pioneer, the finisher." In other words, *the* ultimate standard. This biblical definition is not quite as "convenient" as the above study response would indicate. Rather, our standard and role model, Jesus Christ

Himself, places us on a completely different plane of living—one diametrically opposed to and utterly foreign to that of unbelievers.

Without a standard, there is no sin. Romans tells us this in regard to our Christian lives: "...where there is no law there is no transgression" (4:15).

Without a standard, then, there is no hypocrisy.

So, of course, this means that some of us may be in the clear, for the epidemic of hypocrisy does not apply to the vast pool of sinless Christians.

Good news for robots, bad news for the rest of us!

However, please note the word *perfecter*. Hebrews 12:2 does not say *average, mediocre, marginal, lukewarm, comfortable,* or *complacent.*

The root word is *perfect*. The idea is to shoot for the top, to become more and more like Christ each day. Scripture says we all have missed the mark—that we all have sinned and fallen short of God's ideal (Romans 3:23). We are not intended to be robots who never sin. However, this is actually a moot point if we are truly disciples of Christ seeking to follow His lead.

Imagine training every day for a full year to climb Mount Everest, making a total commitment to accomplishing the feat. Then, as the time for the expedition approaches, you begin to think more anxiously, and doubt creep in. Because the odds are so great that you might fail, you actually *predetermine* that you will turn back before reaching the summit.

Absurd, right? The whole point of training is to *overcome* the odds!

So it is with the Christian expedition of faith. With Oswald Chambers-like abandonment (Chambers, 1992), we go for it and leave the intriguing questions and inane debates in the dust.

We do not look back; we do not look down. We look up, away from ourselves. We follow Christ and invite His Holy Spirit to fill us to overflowing, to go before us, and to surround us on all sides.

The Only Conceivable Remedy

It is this grasp of our own faith that, when shared with others, will produce the type of hypocrites we *want* to be accused of being.

Real faith. Real people. Authentic believers who do sin, but who deal with our sin each day and overcome through Christ our redeemer.

The silver lining slicing through this whole façade of hypocrisy is that *we are forgiven*! If hypocrisy is essentially boiled down to sin, then the great new remedy, the ready-made formula of the year—of a lifetime—is God's forgiveness.

> *I know sometimes people have a reputation for being hypocrites and it frustrates me because we aren't perfect. That's why we need Jesus. People need to look past this. The church has sinners.*
>
> — *Study respondent*

That's right; we are a work in progress. As the bumper sticker says, we aren't perfect, just forgiven. "Being confident of this, that He who began a good work in you will carry it on to completion until the day of Christ Jesus" (Philippians 1:6).

Forgiveness is the difference maker and the building block of the standard we bear. This is why hypocrisy—and the endless accusation of hypocrisy—cannot touch us!

It's what the world will never comprehend, or care enough to.

So we must simply share our stories of forgiveness to help others grasp the freedom that is available to us—as evidenced by Chelsea's story:

> *I was sexually abused from age three. My grandfather, who molested me, kept me only so he could get welfare money to buy whiskey. People said they cared, but did nothing. They would just laugh and talk down at us. We were considered the town drunks. Looking for love and acceptance, I became promiscuous with men and just felt dirtier and dirtier. I hated myself so much that I wanted to commit suicide like my daughter had done. People told me what a sinner I was, but my pastor taught me the love of God who loves me completely and unconditionally. I just want to thank Jesus for loving me and forgiving me even though I am a total sinner. Today, I am telling others about "Jesus, who takes away the sin of the world" (John 1:29).*

Folks, a spade is a spade. According to Scripture, sin is sin. And no matter how you slice it, hypocrisy is sin. The great remedy, the great antidote to cure our mild case of Christianity, is forgiveness—available only through faith in Jesus Christ and the confession of our sin to Him.

Let us together confess that Jesus, perfecter of our faith, is Lord of all, and proclaim that God has raised Him from the dead to vibrantly live in and through us, so that we will individually be reflected to others with the same grace, mercy, and power undeservedly lavished upon us.

CHAPTER SEVEN

"Who Am *I*?"

I made this choice because, at that time in my life,
I had tried to do things my way and got nowhere.
I decided to give my life to God.

— Study Respondent

So, are the problems of hypocrisy and stereotyping greater than God?

Oh, yeah. *God.* Thank heaven, He's still here.

All this talk of hypocrisy, stereotyping, and rejection of the message is merely the Bad News. The Good News is that God is still in the equation, and to a greater extent than we might imagine.

Fact is, when we consider sharing our faith with another person and we become tense and rather unsure of ourselves—and of our message—how quickly we forget God Himself!

The message is unchanging, and the message is His.

Leave it to Him, please.

If we are at all concerned with a potential blow-off, then we're actually giving priority to our own agenda and reputation rather than to representing Christ and pointing people to Him.

So who are we representing, really? Ourselves or God?

But who am I to represent God? You may wonder. If so, you're in good company. When it comes to carrying God's message, many others travel this path of inferiority.

Two cows were in a pasture one day when a milk truck drove by. On the side of the truck was a sign: *Homogenized, Pasteurized, Standardized, Vitamin A Enriched.*

One cow looked at the other and said, "Makes you feel sorta inadequate, doesn't it?"

"Who am I to represent God?" is the very question Moses asked when God visited him at the burning bush. Even after God had singled him out and *chosen* him, Moses too, felt what we feel. Inadequate. Unworthy.

Question 1: "Why Me?" *(Exodus 3:11)*

This first of four questions sets off a direct exchange between man and God. Immediately Moses played to his inadequacies, his inability to carry out the task for a successful mission to please God (Offner, 1981).

We must understand the context here and there is plenty of it because Moses was an old man when this "calling" came upon him. At age forty, he had been an Egyptian prince. But since then, he had been rather humbled, living as a sheepherder in the wilderness for another forty years. Yes, when God calls him, Brother Moses is eighty years old, a sheepherder, and perhaps a bit slim on self-confidence.

Not quite the emblazoned image we have of mighty Moses parting the raging seas.

Question 2: "Who Are You?" *(Exodus 3:13)*

When Moses posed this question, he was saying, "Hey, who are you to tell me I have the ability and authority to move Pharaoh and Egypt?"

And the veiled question beneath his query is, "What shall I say when they ask who sent me?"

Question 3: "What If They Don't Believe Me?" *(Exodus 4:1)*

Hey Moses, what's the big concern here? You mean you're not sure how to explain to the Israelites and others that God Almighty led you to a burning bush that didn't burn up, spoke to you from the flames, then told you to waltz into Egypt armed with only a wooden staff and lead His people out of bondage?

Glad you had a nice trip up the mountain, old man. Now, back to reality.

Question 4: "How Can I Do This with My Poor Speech?" *(Exodus 4:10)*

In his most tangible question, Moses points to his lack of eloquence for the task of delivering the message that would supposedly free his people from four hundred years of suffering. Surely this last, logical plea will restore some reason to God and He will see fit to interview other, more worthy and capable candidates. However, perhaps public speaking ability was not the primary bullet point God was looking for when He reviewed résumés for this position.

Narcissistic Evangelism

Who's kidding whom? Hypocrisy has been around forever, since the standard was set. Cynically speaking, should one's reluctance to carry the message be any different?

In a way, the imperfect messenger is the perfect message carrier. In our brokenness, humanity should be able to relate to us because they experience the same brokenness. Yet society tends to interpret our brokenness as hypocrisy and, instead of bringing us together with culture, our brokenness often becomes a wedge.

So which type of Christian do you wish to be? Nominal or active?

Apathy is sometimes confused with a gentle spirit. Fear is often confused with being a peacemaker. Quietness is mistaken for being nice. Patience, or "waiting on the Lord," can be confused with sitting on our duff. Point is, as Christians we do not have the option of not taking a stand. For if we don't take a stand for Jesus Christ, we are actually the epitome of a hypocrite.

The more I think about our brand of evangelism, the more I'm convinced that we've made evangelism about *us.*

It is narcissism.

Everyone knows that individuals find the notion of sharing the gospel a daunting prospect. What it really should be is a natural outflow of a heart and life yielded to the living Lord Jesus Christ.

But we overthink it. We complicate it. Perhaps we are intimidated by our fear of being rejected as the messenger, or perhaps the adversary, Satan, is preying on our human insecurities.

From this mindset, sharing Christ with others feels more like an obligation than an honor, and it becomes a humanistic type of effort. If we share Christ at all, we basically just want to get it done and feel good about it. Again, for *us.* It becomes more about us and less about the people we're trying to inform of the greatest news ever.

This mentality paves the way for mass personal evangelism—tracts, numbers, notches, and more negative categorizations that substantiate and perpetuate the cycle of stereotyping. But it is up to us to replace the negative images with positive, indelible links in our representation of Christ and our presentation of His message. One man sought to do just that by starting a prayer group within his large company:

I've learned that there are always a lot of reasons not to do something. And while the reasons to move ahead and do it often are elusive, I have also learned that a person of action is rare. Many of the people who attend my prayer group at work are Christians who regularly attend church and who are doing their best to live out their faith in the best way they know how. I've advocated for years the importance of being a person who acts out [his] faith, but I also know that for most it isn't that easy.

So I step forward and I act, and in return I ask others to follow with me and to support the step forward that I am making. That's how community works. When one steps forward, others feel comfortable to step forward, then more come forward and so on. To this day, I know of many of my coworkers who won't come to the prayer group meeting because they are afraid of what it might cost them [at] their job. Without risk, there is no reward.

The risk is far greater inside our minds, though, than it is in actuality. We tend to view it as though we were standing beside Moses and looking at the Red Sea, but the truth of it is that the risk is mostly in our minds. What little risk I incur is by far overcome by the grateful thanks that I regularly receive. There have been those who have sought out our group after having heard of it through the grapevine and have asked us to pray for whatever need they may have.

In the end, the opportunity was created when I stepped forward to be a doer instead of a watcher. This world needs more doers, more risk takers, more people of courage and wisdom who aren't afraid to bring their faith to work with them. God uses the willing.

How many times have we chosen not to share life with someone due to reasons that have nothing to do with God but everything to do with ourselves—or our perception of the person with whom we had the opportunity to speak?

This has nothing to do with the Redeemer Himself; it has everything to do with our own inadequacies. The bottom line is that we, too, often do not trust the message.

But the message never changes.

The Savior never changes.

An old epigram reads, "If you don't feel close to God, then guess who moved?" Perhaps something has moved, or someone has changed, and guess what? It wasn't God.

So the pertinent question is *do we trust God*?

Samsonite Saints

We have become so encumbered with our natural selves—with our fears, hang-ups, failures, and potential failures—that most of us have great difficulty shedding our inhibitions about sharing the Good News of Jesus Christ.

Does the church really understand that "perfect loves casts out all fear"?

Do you and I begin to grasp the full meaning of God's love for us?

Maybe we do not fully grasp, accept, and absolutely cling to His forgiveness. Although our wounds may be primarily self-inflicted, we are a bruised and battered bunch. This is because we do not fully trust or grasp the incredible fact that when Christ said, "It is finished" from the cross, our sin really was—and is—no more.

In the movie *The Mission*, Robert DeNiro played a character, Rodrigo, who literally bore a wooden cross on his back as penance for his sin. For the first hour of the movie, it's as if the audience feels Rodrigo's burden with him. He is relentless in his devotion as well as in his self-punishment. It was touching and tragic at the same time: touching because Rodrigo is sincere in his regret, but tragic in that we, as followers of Christ, know that such measures are extreme and unnecessary.

But there's something about our sense of guilt as humans—as sinners—that is difficult to grasp or explain, and this was epitomized by the scene in which Rodrigo, his burden released when he sends the cross tumbling down a mountainside, actually runs down the hill after it. This is symbolic of how many of us often carry grief, fear, melancholy, bitterness, unforgiveness, and unrepented sin for far longer than necessary. It's as if we just don't want to give it up, or we have a mental or spiritual block about doing so.

A pastor friend was counseling a woman who had been battling deep depression, and after many sessions she was still experiencing doubt about Christ's desire to release her from this burden. She struggled with whether the promise of the Bible applied to her. At one point, she got up from her chair and walked over to the window of the pastor's office, gazed out wistfully into the sunshine, and said, "But I've lived with it for so long, it's like my best friend."

It's difficult, maybe impossible, to live in peace and joy—and to attract others to a vibrant love relationship with God—when you're trudging under the pile of your own condemnation, guilt, fear, sin, and shame. That's a huge load of unnecessary baggage!

The reality is that as Christians, we're privy to extremely valuable information—more valuable than insider trading secrets or proprietary technological codes. But what we know is far from illegal. It's actually a pathway to freedom. Yet we sit on it, and we decide not to share it. The fashion in which Christendom has botched the opportunity to tell others this life-changing information is nothing short of staggering. It is a bazooka blast to the collective foot of the Body of Christ.

Sometimes, indeed, the enemy is us.

CHAPTER  EIGHT

"I Am"

When you're twenty, you care what everyone thinks about you.
When you're forty, you don't care what anyone thinks about you.
When you're sixty, you realize nobody was ever thinking about you.

— *Dr. Paul Walker*

Does the story of Moses help us rationalize our own reluctance or apathy toward sharing the gospel?

Moses' questions to and about God show a certain lack of trust, which we can see mirrored in our own lives nearly every day. Even when we think we are close to the Lord, we tend to forget Him when faced with circumstances that do not conform to our conditional brand of Christianity. It's easy to do: Sometimes we just lose focus on our leader. Even two friends of Jesus, clouded with doubt that He had risen from the dead, didn't recognize Him when He approached them on their walk to Emmaus (see Luke 24:13-35).

But Moses takes the cake in this regard. When you and I come away from a powerful worship service, we usually feel strong and courageous in the faith. Just imagine how Moses must have felt coming away from the burning bush! Invincible—a veritable tower of faith. The man had literally been *in the presence of God*. Not a feeling, not the emotional heart-tug of a praise song, but the very presence of God Almighty!

And still, he had the audacity and lack of faith to question God.

Why?

I think primarily because Moses thought the mission was about him. Just as we do, Moses did not see the *calling*; he missed it right out of the gate. The trees in his own forest of doubt and self-concern clouded his vision, causing him to question God's ability to transcend his inadequacies for the greater purpose. As Karen's remarks exemplify, our "mission" isn't necessarily in a foreign country. It can be right in front of us:

> *I'm comfortable in my "missionary skin" because I know that I wouldn't be doing it if God hadn't tasked me with such a ministry, and I have come to believe that my mission is right where I am. So, I am a missionary. I am a stranger in a strange land and I'm really kind of okay with that. As I go to and fro in my life, I bring my faith along with me. Even though the people of my community already have clean drinking water, plenty of food, and a place to worship, they need missionaries who are willing to bring along their faith and walk alongside them. That's what a missionary does.*

> *Maybe to some people the word missionary seems like a lofty word, but to me it means that I have a purpose in Christ. It means that each day that I live out my purpose is a day that my mission thrives and is blessed by the God I serve. My mission is to serve people—and in doing so, to serve God. I believe that you are a missionary, too. Maybe you haven't realized it or maybe you have, but I believe that God has a mission for everyone, but not everyone is willing. Be willing and I believe you will be called to [your own] mission field.*

God had been preparing Moses for service. How did Moses respond to the call?

Today's followers of Christ have an even greater calling, a command to take God's message to the ends of the earth (Matthew 28:18-20).

How will we respond to the call?

When God calls, we can *react* or we can *respond*. Moses perfectly displays a very natural, human reaction—immediate and impulsive.

"Who Am I?"

This was the first question Moses asked. We tend to pose the same question when God asks us to carry His message to others in desperate need of living water. If we brush others off, concealing our life-giving stories, we virtually keep the focus on ourselves by the implicit question, "Why me, Lord? Who am I to do this?" We know the question well. It entails all our excuses, rationalizations, inadequacies, and reluctance.

"Who am *I*? Why me, Lord?" is a false humility, a convenient excuse to avoid God's call until we find out exactly who we are. No matter how you slice it, whether as old-school inadequacy or New Age self-worship, "Why me?" is a reaction of fear and an avoidance of preparation for the call. When it comes to obeying God and following His guidance, fear of our shortcomings and focusing on our search for self are rooted in pride. Therefore, if we fail to follow through on the Great Commission, we are just as hypocritical as anyone else.

"Who Are You (and Can I Trust You)?"

Moses' second question was a backdoor way of asking God, "Who are *You*?" In Jewish culture, a name meant something deeper about a person's character or inner nature. So this question really approaches God about His character and whether He can keep His promises.

In the same way, we also have the audacity to ask God, "Who are You (and can I trust You)?" We ask this implicitly in our attitudes such as doubt, fear, and worry. We also ask it directly, for example, when we make decisions without consulting the Lord. Both are signs of an internal power struggle for sole control of our lives. As our society moves further away from the concept of a personal God and increasingly toward an absorption with self, the question "Who are You and can I trust You?" may also characterize the cry of the current generation.

> *The world system encourages you to be your best, not so much because that will enable you to help more people, but because then you have something to be proud about so you can feel good about yourself.*

> — Study Respondent

"What If They Don't Believe Me?"

Of course, we are masters of Moses' third question, which is essentially, "What will people think?" More than anything, Moses' story shows that human weakness and pride are always at direct and combative odds with the Spirit of God within us. Standing in the actual presence of the Lord, Moses is still concerned about what other people may think and say if he tries to represent God as boldly as God commands. With our eyes fixed on ourselves, our human tendency is to do the same as Moses: dodge and avoid. And if avoidance doesn't work, then by all means let's protect our reputation and pride.

This is precisely what Moses was concerned with. What he was really seeking was validation. He wanted some credentials to flash to show that he was representing someone or something greater than himself. God answers Moses' third question by providing three signs he can use to convince the people that his mission is of God.

At times, of course, God provides signs along the journey for us as well. But we must never allow our need for "signs of God's will" to substitute for basic trust in Him. Here is the key issue: Is this about *us*, or about something far greater than we are? Do others see fear, hesitancy, and hypocrisy, or does our very countenance reveal credentials for delivering a message that transcends time, space, and humanity itself?

Moses raises the "What will people think?" question because he's concerned over his inadequate speaking ability. He wonders, *How can I pull this off without being eloquent or articulate?* We raise similar smokescreens when faced with opportunities to share life with others, bemoaning our lack of scriptural knowledge and convincing ourselves that surely someone else can better relate with a particular person or group.

Moses has the sheer audacity to ask this question of the very Creator God who made him. God's wonderful reply to Moses was "Who made your mouth?" That could be applied to any and every excuse we can fathom today. When we question God as directly as Moses did about our ability or lack thereof, we take the interchange to a different level by actually criticizing God. In effect, we limit Him in our thinking, placing Him in a box.

So here is the order of events:

1. God made us.

2. We made a box.

3. We put God in our box.

We expect Him to do what *we* want Him to do *whenever* we want it done.

A colleague of mine loves to tell stories about his one-year-old son, Beau, who is not quite walking or talking, but can still get in plenty of trouble. In terms of the way we oftentimes regard God, we're like toddlers. A toddler like Beau is incapable of taking care of himself, and even incapable of speaking. When a toddler needs something or wants something, he points, gets emphatic, and/or cries in order to get what he wants. What the toddler doesn't understand is that the parent already intends to provide the toddler everything he needs in order to grow up healthy and strong. No amount of stomping and crying will change the mindset of a loving, confident parent in terms of meeting the true needs of that toddler.

We must step out of our own personal experience and let God out of the box! The challenge for us is to acknowledge and remove what we feel is standing in the way of what God wants to do through us.

No amount of stomping or crying will make God love us any more or any less. That's why it's so difficult for us to fully understand the concept of unconditional love, especially God's unconditional love.

The Answers

For our purposes, the answers to Moses' first two questions have the greatest impact. Even the great Moses questioned his own capacity and ability to serve and speak for God. We essentially ask or question God in the same way when He asks us to be witnesses directly for Him: "But God, who am I?"

God answers this question by simply stating, "I will be with you." Grasping this profound statement comes with an understanding of *calling*. A call is really a disruption. At age eighty, God's call on Moses was a disruption of a volcanic proportion. Feeling pulled and stretched from different directions is common during a call. We do not grow by simply going the same way. During seasons such as these, we must differentiate between personal conviction and God's "conviction" or purpose for us.

After finishing seminary, I was still well south of age thirty and had plenty of personal conviction (and ego) to try to become a "tentmaker" overseas as a pro or semi-pro basketball player. Through prayer and practicality, I learned that this was not God's purpose for me. And frankly, it hurt a bit. Sometimes the Lord will use the most practical ramifications to make the way clearer for us. In this case, it was clear that folks were not beating down my door to pay me to play basketball abroad.

Shortly thereafter, I was led to begin a ministry in the United States incorporating my passions for Christian music and sports evangelism. Where my original vision focused mainly on basketball, God expanded my vision into His. And because He knows my heart better than I do, He graciously chose to include my passion for music in His expanded plan. The ministry included concert promotion and a syndicated modern Christian music show for college radio. Had I played pro basketball in Europe, I may never have experienced the joys of reaching people through Christian music.

God promises that if we fulfill His call by doing what He says, He will be with us. In Matthew 28:20, after Jesus commanded His disciples to witness for Him throughout the world, He added this promise and blessing: "…and surely I am with you always, to the very end of the age."

Yet, as we've seen, recent surveys show that only 35 percent of us feel any responsibility to tell others about our faith. The inverse means that 65 percent of us consider these words of Jesus to be the Great Suggestion instead of the Great Commission.

A professing Christian in our study offers this view:

> Christianity is important to my life. It helps to give meaning and purpose to my life. I don't accept that I should practice "The Great Commission." Everyone doesn't need saving. People should choose what is right for them.

We must respond to Jesus' call, thrusting aside all the deceit, self-doubt, worry, fear, reluctance, pride—any barrier that impedes us from carrying out the will and calling of God. Instead of an impulsive, defensive *reaction* soaked in self-absorption, ours is to be the *response* of a lifetime—for a lifetime.

Ever wonder why fellow believers—even pastors, leaders, and missionaries—experience burn-out from service? They simply outrun the power cord. When we respond to the call in a way that is sincere and yielded to the Holy Spirit, we ensure that we're connected to our source of power—God, who has promised never to leave us nor forsake us.

Staying plugged in. Abiding in Him, and Him in us, allows us to truly *know* with all our being that God is with us. This is the place of faith in which our self-concerned fears begin to be displaced by God-breathed confidence, tempered by humility.

And above all, this is the real take-home lesson of the Moses story: that despite his inadequacy and lack of self-confidence, Moses' faith would grow exponentially because he responded obediently to the call. An ordinary man—a sheepherder—responds to the call, abides in God, and accomplishes extraordinary miracles...finally freeing his people from captivity and leading them to the borders of the Promised Land. The key ingredient: confidence tempered by humility.

Just as Moses saw God turn his fear into humble confidence, we can also gain humble confidence by taking three crucial steps when God calls us:

1. Obey.

2. Act.

3. Watch the proof unfold.

The proof that Moses was truly called was evidenced by the results of his obedience.

Distinguishing between missional success and the more-important result of obedience is foreign to our society. Closer to the heart of God and His calling is the obedience it takes, regardless of the outcome, to relinquish our fear and trust completely in the Lord, who promises to be with us. Throughout these questions of doubt from Moses, we see that God is attentive, and more importantly, *sufficient* for any weakness that we may bring to the table. The fine line I most appreciate here is that God reassures us up to a point, and then He expects faith and obedience on our part. Even throughout forty years in the wilderness, God proved His faithfulness to the Israelites. As He was with them in the wilderness, He is with us in our own wildernesses, as Steven testifies:

> *I understand the meaning of loneliness. My mom and dad loved me, but deep inside something was missing. Church, to me, was a word, not a relationship. When I left home at the age of nineteen, I went to school, wasted my money like the Prodigal Son, and turned to the party scene. It was while I was working at a restaurant that a girl invited me to church. There I had my first encounter with the reality*

> of Jesus Christ and gave my heart to Him. I have been placed in a
> greater family now, with the Holy Spirit, who will never leave me. I
> have come home to the loving arms of the Father.

In Exodus 3:13, Moses has the nerve to ask God, "What shall I say
when they ask me the name of this God who sent me?"

God answers by saying, "I AM WHO I AM. This is what you are to
say to the Israelites: 'I AM has sent me to you'" (v. 14). And in the
next verse, God adds, "Say to the Israelites, 'The LORD, the God of
Abraham, the God of Isaac and the God of Jacob, has sent me to you.'
This is my name forever, the name by which I will be remembered
from generation to generation."

These two verses are an extraordinary foundation for the authentic
Christian life, out of which will flow the type of witness that will
naturally affect others. It's as close to a specific antidote to hypocrisy
and stereotyping as we can get, as we're assured that God is both a
personal God and the God of history.

In this unique exchange between Moses and God, we see that God
is so much greater than Moses' excuses. It's a bit like child's play.
God answers Moses' reluctance to speak by reminding him that
He gave Moses the very mouth with which *to* speak—He created
him. He wants us to have His perspective, not our limited human
perspectives—for when our thinking is in line with God's, our minds
are not on ourselves. We are focused on Him and Him alone, and on
what He can do in us and through us to help others. With God in us,
our human fears and inadequacies become irrelevant.

And…we finally realize that genuinely *helping* others is often far
better than *evangelizing* others. We know (from Abraham Maslow
and others) that only after the basic needs of a human being are met is

he or she then more ready, willing, and able to comprehend a spoken message—especially one of a spiritual nature.

So as we contemplate this story from Exodus, we can begin to see how God might have been chuckling at Moses as the eighty-year-old shepherd tried to squirm his way out of such a calling. Moses' trepidation is illustrative of the many times you and I have played hide and seek from God to justify and rationalize our poor behavior or tepid witness for Him. "Wimping out" is so very easy to do, but in God's eyes it is a colossal charade. When God calls us to a task, He also enables and empowers us with what we need to accomplish the task. When God calls, we have no legitimate excuses.

"Who the heck am *I?*" we ask.

And God answers, "I will be with you because I AM WHO I AM."

He says this from a position that we just cannot fathom—that of the eternal, omnipotent, omnipresent Creator and Lord of the universe.

Imagine a mother sitting her daughter down for a pre-marriage chat and explaining the intricacies of maintaining a mature, committed relationship…before her daughter's first day in kindergarten. The mother has so much knowledge that the daughter hasn't even considered yet, things that are pointless to bring up at this point in the little girl's life. Mom's message is completely beyond the daughter's limited perspective and life experience.

Explaining God's plan—or even God's love—is something that oftentimes is beyond our limited level of comprehension.

Our God is a personal God, but He is also a God of history. In fact, He precedes history—He was here before any other existence. Talk about "been there, done that!" Therefore, our comprehension of God is limited because we view Him from our own thinking, from within our own narrow, personal life experience. But, being God, He is so vastly bigger than:

- *time...* for He is not limited to time as we are, nor is He compelled to meet our personal timetable;

- *space...* for there's nowhere He can't go, and nothing He can't see. He is a broad-minded God;

- *context...* for God works in other people, other churches, and other countries in ways we cannot even imagine.

He is a God of history because He existed before time. With this perspective in mind, we can better understand that God may chuckle at the petty excuses and smokescreens we offer Him. And when it comes to meeting the challenges we've been talking about, God is greater than they are. He's greater than our hypocrisy. He's greater than society's stereotyping. He just is.

Part of God's greatness is His incredible love that enables Him to listen to our lame excuses, yet not belittle us. Instead of condescendingly replying to Moses that He created Moses and the universe as well, God reminds Moses of His faithfulness to other individuals who had come before him. So in His wisdom, He allows Moses to exercise his own faith—faith God knew Moses would need in the task that lay ahead of him. This is *the* superior model of relating—and of contextualizing our message—one to one, person-to-person.

The big picture is never bigger than *one* heart. This is why the reformation from hypocrisy must occur with one heart and one life at a time. From this story we learn that there are no spiritual giants, only faithful, flawed people like Moses. We cannot expect an overnight recovery, but rather an arduous journey through the wilderness. The journey begins with real, faithful people. The journey begins in the mirror—with you and with me. Mahatma Gandhi said, "We must become the change we want to see."

Flawed but faithful.

The God of Abraham, Isaac, and Jacob has been evident and active in the lives of others throughout history. Even with Moses, as great a historical figure as he is, God reached out individually, recognizing Moses' every shortcoming, need, and desire. This is how God deals with His children: carefully, lovingly, and with wisdom beyond our comprehension. He wants to be and do the same within us. If we will only abandon our excuses, set aside our addiction to mediocrity, and fully embrace His call, we can walk faithfully and confidently with the great I AM.

CHAPTER NINE

The Bridge to Square One

"I AM the Alpha and the Omega," says the Lord God, "who is, and who was, and who is to come, the Almighty"

— Revelation 1:8

Christianity has gotten into a habit of starting to tell our story in the middle instead of at the beginning. This has brought about a situation in which we continually lose our audience because of a lack of proper "context." There is a reason that a story has a beginning, a middle, and an end—to understand the answers at the end, the audience must understand the beginning.

Christ was sent to earth so that mankind could find the road back to God's original intent. In today's post-Christian culture, the questions people ask revolve around themselves, as in: "Who am I?", "Why am I here?", "What am I supposed to do?", and "Where am I going?" So to ask someone, "Who is Jesus?" or "Have you accepted Jesus as your Savior?" really only makes sense to the hearers when asked in the context of their self-focused questions.

> *I do not subscribe to the belief that a supreme being controls my fate.*
>
> *— Study respondent*

> *I wasn't born into a religion and I don't believe any one of them holds the truth.*
>
> *— Study respondent*

The Greatest Story's Author

In order for the great news of God's forgiveness to make sense to our culture, we *must* take both the message, and the hearer, back to the Greatest Story's author. Back to God.

Remember God's self-description? I AM. When Moses asked God, "Who shall I say sent me?" God replied, "Tell them I AM sent you."

What does this mean ... I AM? Ponder this. Really ponder it. Do Christians, even disciples of Jesus Christ, know the inexplicably deep meaning of God's statement about Himself? If we do not, then how much *more* clueless are unbelievers about the concept of the great I AM? Without God, there is no creation. No Eden. No man, woman, animals, vegetation, water, skies, sun, moon, or stars. No intelligence, creativity, or free will. There is nothing but nothing.

All of those exist because God exists. "I AM." He *is*. Always was, always will be. We're here because He loves us and wants close fellowship with us.

But we blew it. We misused our gift of free will to rebel against Him. He is so righteous that He cannot look upon our sin, so our sin separated us from our loving, longing heavenly Father.

But we need Him as much as He longs for us. As French physicist and philosopher Blaise Pascal wrote, "There is a God-shaped vacuum in the heart of each man that cannot be filled by any created thing, but only by God, the Creator, made known through His Son, Jesus Christ."

Without God, and our acknowledgment of our sinful state, there is no need for:

- Sacrifice for atonement of sin.

- Redemption.

- The New Covenant.

- Jesus.

- The cross.

- Jesus' death.

- His resurrection.

Take a look at where we are as a society. Every single day of our lives, in no uncertain terms, Madison Avenue tells us that we must have exactly what we want when we want it. Not later, not next week, but right now. Far too often, God is viewed as an inhibitor of what we want. It's more convenient to our lifestyle to make God whoever we need Him to be at the moment.

This convenient concept of "God is whoever you need Him to be" can be seen in all sorts of man-made belief systems:

- Paganism.

- Esotericism.

- Nihilism.

- New Age.

- Humanism.

- Neo-Paganism.

- Relativism.

- Same old cults.

- Dangerous new cults.

> *I believe that the "gods" in all religions are the same. They just appear in different forms for different people.*
>
> — Study respondent

Meanwhile, what has seemingly disintegrated into vapor in our hearts and minds is the definition Jesus gives of Himself in John 14:6:

I AM...

The Way...

The Truth...

The Life.

No one comes to the Father [God] but through me.

Jesus Christ is God's only provision for our sin. He is the only way to the Father. He is the sole mediator—the bridge—between God and man (1 Timothy 2:5). While modern society deems this "only way" mindset "intolerance," God calls it "love." Jesus demonstrated ultimate love through His sacrificial death on the cross for our sin.

God does not change. He doesn't need to. He's *God*. Always wise, always relevant. Always omniscient and omnipotent and omnipresent. He doesn't take opinion polls or alter His ways depending on the mood of the world. God is the same yesterday, today, and forever.

But ...

> *I've studied different religions and personal metaphysical experiences, and combined the concepts that best fit together as well as the native beliefs I learned from my family.*
>
> — Study respondent

I believe that man's destiny is a ship steered by the course of environment and one's own actions. It is not by some mysterious guy in the sky.

— *Study respondent*

...we came across these sentiments often in our study. Our world tries so hard to believe in *everything* that, in the end, they believe in *nothing*.

Standing for nothing.

Offending no one.

Tolerant of everything except those they intolerantly dub "intolerant."

The Cult of Self-Worship

This is most evident in the self-worship of contemporary society. Today, as throughout history, mankind avoids God and worships many other things: image, money, fame, celebrities, sports figures, and possessions. But the majority of our devotion is to ourselves. *Self* is not only the name of a popular magazine—it is our golden calf.

"Why do we need God? Just look within yourself—you have the power to overcome!"

It's just a recycled lie, a twenty-first century angle on the ancient root of it all: paganism. In fact, modern theologians have dubbed it *neo-paganism*. In a nutshell, neopaganism is the worship of anything other than the true God, the creator and Lord of the universe. As Kathleen shares, neopaganism is a very cheap substitute for the truth:

After years in radical feminism, Wicca, Hare Krishna, leftist politics and affairs with married professors, I bought into New Ageism and then finally began following an Indian guru and converted to Hinduism. I wore a sari, put a red bindi spot on my head, chanted in Sanskrit, and lived in an ashram. I nearly killed myself thinking that I was a "Star Child" with "infinite human potential" and the power to "create my own reality." WHAT A CROCK!

The greatest day of my life came when I discovered that I, like everyone else, was a hopeless sinner unable to do the simplest things to save myself. God loved me just as I was and Jesus was the prescription. Jesus was the cure. I asked Him into my life and I ask you to do the same.

Substitutes for Truth

What does the average person think of God?

Of course, we are a biblically illiterate society, and the same may be applied to the church. We do not know theology. And I am not talking about seminary knowledge, but the actual study of God.

Who is He? Why is He?

As we've seen, even the great Moses had such questions. If a man of God like Moses directed such queries straight to God in His very presence, imagine the numerous questions from individuals in our generation.

Yes, I changed from Christianity. It could not answer my questions satisfactorily—and being African, it left me with more questions. Also, most Christians don't act in a way that is in accordance with Christ. They preach.

— Study respondent

Though we may espouse God, we do not know God.

Which means, of course, that we struggle against preconceptions, misconceptions, mispresentations, and misrepresentations of the *message*. I don't think we have the first clue what is in the head, and more importantly, in the *heart* of an unbeliever—the doubt, fear, disillusionment, or even anger that must exude from within.

In a world this difficult and frustrating, is there really such a thing as self-sufficiency? Romans 1:20 states, "For since the creation of the world God's invisible qualities—his eternal power and divine nature— have been clearly seen, being understood from what has been made, so that people are without excuse." Can one really feel completely comfortable functioning as a self-contained entity without belief in God? It's certainly a choice a lot of people make. Considering this scripture, it would seem that the people who seem difficult to reach may be the ones closest to God's heart. These people are dearly loved, and we must view them as only a touch away. And we must not forget that, as astonishing as it may be, God uses us as His hands.

There are moments when I have truly felt God's presence and how indescribable a close walk with the true I AM really is. In these moments it's as though I'm overwhelmed with the simplicity of what really matters to Him. He wants us to believe, trust, and follow Him. He wants *relationship*, while we want *religion*. It's as if we seek rules or barriers to insulate ourselves from an actual relationship with our Creator. Got-tos and can't-dos. Church buildings. Entertaining programs. Preachers, teachers, administrators, youth pastors, event coordinators. Bulletins and newsletters. Websites. Literature. Books. Books. Books.

When I humble myself at the feet of God and listen, really listen, I feel that most Christians have it precisely, 180 degrees backward. At least I do.

Religion is a substitute for truth. It clouds intimacy with our Lord. Jesus detested religion. After all, religion wasn't doing the Pharisees and Sadducees any good—they were so intent on "doing religion" that they totally missed out on the truth...and on personal intimacy with the heavenly Father.

Author Edward Cell contends that religion often functions as a substitute for relationship with God. This is particularly true, for example, when one uses the term "God" to refer to the idol of self-interest. Cell makes this bold and revealing statement regarding religion and contemporary culture: "Religion, in effect, may itself be a leading expression of the death of God." I couldn't agree more. Have we allowed *religion* (and all the baggage that comes with it) to cloud what God really wants, which is *relationship*?

When the traditions of old men collide with the humanistic, why-would-we-need-God mentality thinking of new men, it sets a course for disaster that will never arrive at truth. As John Stott remarked in an address to students and faculty at Wycliffe College in Toronto, "The great tragedy in the church today is that evangelicals are biblical but not contemporary, while liberals are contemporary but not biblical. We need faithfulness to the ancient word and sensitivity to the modern world."

Comfort, Dissonance, and Resentment

While many churches today are seemingly focused on buildings, programs, flash, and splash to impress contemporary society, our study responses say something different about where the focus should be directed. Our question was: *If you were to hear the content of this presentation again, where (in which setting), and how (through which medium) would you be most open to hearing it?* The key word summarizing the responses to this question was *comfort.* Respondents seem to be more concerned about being comfortable with the people and with the presenter of the message than with the venue or program.

We are currently in the age of "Social ADD" (Attention Deficit Disorder). This generation has grown up in a culture where if they don't like something, they simply change the channel. But with the advent of texts and Tweets and Facebook, the entire world can hear a story, comment on it, and move to the next thing all in a matter of minutes. Not only are the attention spans of our audience diminishing, but when people perceive dissonance in the Christian message they're likely to employ defensive tactics as quickly as one changes a television channel via remote control.

Today's men and women are so accustomed to having what they want when they want it that being uncomfortable in a religious setting, where they are not required to be, will certainly lead to dissonance and, as some have reported, resentment. As one respondent replied to the question of where and how he would be most open to hearing the gospel message: *None. I don't want to hear it.*

Religion or Relationship?

Religion, through its own human effort (programs, institution, formats, ritual) has in many cases supplanted personal relationship and discipleship. We go to church and follow programs which are designed to sort of *help* God nurture us, and when we finish programs 101, 102, 103, we should be "fit and healthy" Christians. Consequently, as another respondent underscored, the institution and structure of modern religion can often supersede cultural relevance:

I was raised by my Christian parents in the church and never really thought much of it. Church was a boring place I was forced to go to on Sundays and miss some good cartoons. My parents made no effort to make me believe in Santa or the Easter Bunny, but they did convince me that there was a god (which I still believe, but it sure ain't the one I was raised to believe in). That was kind of the end of it for a while, nothing really changed, and I still didn't see much point to church— why would God care about me going to a stupid building? But I was shut up by the threat of no longer receiving Christmas presents.

Billy Graham has said that on any given Sunday, 75 percent of the people in the pews of American's churches have no personal relationship with Jesus Christ. As one Christian respondent admonished:

Believing in God is something that I do not or will never regret. But just being "religious" is not going to get you anywhere. You have to know God on a personal level.

Please don't get me wrong. I am 100 percent for the church…the way Jesus intended the church to be. The Scriptures urge us to not forsake gathering together with fellow believers for prayer, devotion, Scripture reading, teaching, preaching, fellowship, baptism, communion, and outreach. But these components of the Christian walk are even more powerful when implemented in our own personal relationships with the Lord, which should be 24/7/365 instead of once or twice a week.

Then, when we do come together as believers, we are all the more enhanced, equipped, and edified by one another. Between gatherings, however, what's the quality level of our personal time communing with God and soaking in His Word? Have we who call ourselves Christians lost the concept of personal piety, a perpetual hunger and thirst for more of God and for greater intimacy and fellowship with Jesus Christ?

That's what is real when it comes to the Greatest Story Ever Told. Religion is not the real thing. Neither is the institution. The only real thing is God, the great I AM, and the amazing love He demonstrated by giving His only Son, Jesus Christ, so that whoever believes in Him should not perish, but have everlasting life.

Jesus: the Bridge to God, the Bridge Builder

To be better, truer, more authentic tellers of the Greatest Story, we must *point people to Jesus* and *away* from ourselves. He is the bridge between sinful man and our loving, righteous God. But people cannot fathom the bridge without first considering, pondering, and longing for the bridge builder—God Himself.

The heavenly Father.

I AM.

This is square one.

God, the loving Creator, started it all. He made us for fellowship with Him. But because of our sin, humankind is separated from God. But because of God's nature as the embodiment of righteousness, He cannot overlook sin. However, He loved us so much that He gave His only Son as the permanent sacrifice for our sin, so that all who trust and believe in Jesus can enjoy fellowship with God now and forever.

That's love.

That's our God.

That's square one.

Through His Son, Jesus, God bridged the chasm between sinful man and righteous God. The Greatest Story is that because of His amazing love for us, we can look Jesus straight in His eye, open our hearts to Him, and take the step of faith across the bridge of reconciliation with God.

> *I have made this choice because I believe each person has an innate desire to fill an emptiness inside. Jesus Christ fills and completes.*
>
> —*Study respondent*

CHAPTER TEN

Do We Really Know Who We Are?

The gospel is that humans are inherently sinful.
Nothing we can ever do will make us righteous in the eyes of God.
Therefore, a perfect human that is outside the normal set of humans
is needed to bridge the gap between the human world and God.
That bridge is Jesus Christ, and it serves as the
only connection between humans and God.

— *Study respondent*

Who are you in the eyes of God?

Who are you in your own eyes? In the eyes of others?

In today's world we are mostly identified by our country, state, city, job, school, church, and family. These foundational elements may describe us to an extent, but they do not speak directly to our character, to the persons we are.

After we acknowledge God—His person, His attributes, His love—only then can we begin to grasp who we are, in His eyes, in ours, and in the eyes of others. Our foundation is God. Our identity is in His Son, Jesus Christ.

Identity in Christ

God never intended for us to live *for* Him; rather, He created us to live *in* Him. His intention is not for us to imitate Him, but to abide in Him and allow Him to live in and through us.

> *I have been crucified with Christ and I no longer live, but Christ lives in me. The life I live in the body, I live by faith in the Son of God, who loved me and gave himself for me.*
>
> —*Galatians 2:20*

This is the whole point of the incarnation: God sending His holy Son to earth to become a human being, like us, experiencing the real stuff of life and showing us the way. Because of this identification, we can, in turn, be identified in Christ Jesus.

First Corinthians 15 speaks of two men: the first Adam and the second Adam. The first Adam brought disobedience; the second brought a New Covenant—a new life. Is our identity in the nature of the first man, or in the nature of the second man?

Like the two-sided costume with two faces suggests, we often try to ride the fence between these two natures. As Chelsea describes, seeking to please only ourselves and those around us can lead to personal despair and anguish:

> *I love God more than anything. Years ago I stopped going to church. Bad things happened and I fell farther and farther away. Now, I look to Him and I still get answers, but I don't feel Him like I used to. I crave the love I once had. I blamed Him for everything, and sometimes I feel like even begging for mercy isn't enough. I messed up not just my life, but that of my best friend. I got her into a lot of things, and I ruined her relationship with God. And now I feel like, how can He still love me when I hurt one of His most faithful children? I love Him and I just wish I knew that He knew how much. I desire to be closer to Him. But how?*

In the ultimate substitution, God sent His only Son, who was without sin, to actually *become* sin for each of us so that we might become the righteousness of God (see 2 Corinthians 5:21). We who receive Christ as our personal Savior and Lord actually died *in* Him and *with* Him on the cross. So we are dead to sin and alive *in* Him.

Our true identity is all about the unveiling of who we are in Him and through Him. "Who God is" must come first, then "who we are" follows.

In whom are we abiding? Are we abiding in Adam, in ourselves, or in Christ?

If we abide in the first Adam, in the sinful state of mankind without accepting the redemption of God's Son, we will also decay and die. The problem is not our sins (plural); but *sin* (singular)—the sinful state of unredeemed mankind.

In the same way, we have traced the root of hypocrisy to *ongoing sin.*

Sin makes us self-aware and self-conscious, rather than God-aware and God-conscious. If we abide in Adam's state or our own selfish state, we're the perfect breeding ground for hypocrisy.

Instead of newsworthy "public" sins, this is a subtle, daily temptation beckoning to open the door to ongoing sin. This is precisely why each one of us is susceptible to hypocrisy.

The Battle

Torn by a constant, inner tug-of-war between spirit and flesh, we are in the midst of a war. Though we have explicit equipment and marching orders given in Ephesians 6, we are often oblivious to the battles being waged on our behalf. Why? Because we have not grounded ourselves with the proper spiritual armor and mindset to step up boldly and defeat the enemy.

Many of us don't understand who we are in Christ. It is difficult to grasp that He who is *in you* is greater than he who is in the world. So the fight against hypocrisy—sin—is actually a fight against that which is unlike Jesus Christ within us, that which is inconsistent with Him and His character. When we sin, we are being disloyal to our new nature, which is Jesus Christ within us.

But it is vital to realize that we are absolutely never alone in this fight. However, our human nature tends to want to go it alone, to not appropriate the incredible power available to us from God's Holy Spirit. As Roger's story illustrates, we sometimes tend to shy away from even the thought of God, as though we have to be squeaky-clean in order to approach Him for forgiveness.

> *Unfortunately, I'm at a place in my life where I'm not living it as I feel I should. Knowing this, and feeling too weak to change my course at the moment, I'm loath to go to church. How can I face God if I'm sinning in my heart and in action? Last week, I did something so outrageous, even for me, that it propelled me to church for the first time in about a decade.*
>
> *The message that day was interesting: Don't avoid church because you're weak or wounded. When you're struggling and you know you're doing wrong, that's the time you need God the most—and He knows what you're doing anyway. Since you can't hide it from Him, you're only hiding from yourself. You might as well come home.*

Honesty with ourselves and with God is a fundamental first step in rejecting hypocrisy and completely embracing our identity in Christ. It's not as simple as saying, "I'm just not going to sin" or "I'm going to sin because I'm human; there isn't much I can do about it." Each of these statements deny the powers of both the flesh and the Spirit.

It is Satan's objective to confuse us about the truth of Christ in us. After all, we're all imperfect and we all sin. Satan preys upon our own self-doubt and our inability to overcome sin (Romans 7:19). The deception happens subtly, one day at a time. When we lose focus on Christ and cease abiding in Him, we begin to lose the battle. Before we know it, we're living like everyone else. Satan wants us to feel separated from God and, not so coincidentally, sin is exactly what separates us from God.

Christ is the bridge between sinful man and righteous God. So if Satan can confuse us about who we are in Christ—getting us to think that Christ is only in us *if* we are free from sin—then he has us wrapped around his finger. The truth is that for followers of Jesus Christ, He is *always* in us. The Scriptures tell us that our bodies are the temple of His Holy Spirit. But we don't always remember or acknowledge that fact and the incredible power that comes with it; we don't allow Him to be fully God.

Being hypocritical ignores Christ's Spirit within us and places us out of fellowship with Him. But yielding to His Spirit's power to reject hypocrisy declares to the enemy, and to the world, that we embrace Christ and all that He is, and that we want our attitudes, words, and actions to bring honor and glory to Him.

The Cure: It Is Finished

If hypocrisy is a "cancer"—and our data underscores that *it is*—then we must get back in the "lab" and find the cure.

Hebrews 12 gives believers a sound, step-by-step strategy to combat and overcome hypocrisy. The chapter begins by exhorting us to throw off everything that hinders, including the sin that so easily entangles us, and to run with perseverance and keep our eyes on Jesus, the author and perfecter of our faith. The third verse challenges us to consider Him who endured scorn and opposition so that we won't grow weary and lose heart. The scorn, shame, and persecution that Jesus endured was more than we can ever imagine facing in our society.

There is a difference between persecution and prejudice. One actually has to take a bold stand in order to be persecuted. Though there have been increasing occurrences of persecution in North America, for the most part our continent cannot even speak to this. In America we are truly spoiled when it comes to the freedom to speak about and practice our beliefs. What we do experience is prejudice. Often just by the nature of being grouped and stereotyped, Christian people are, ironically, judged by those who accuse us of being narrow-minded and judgmental.

"In your struggle against sin, you have not resisted to the point of shedding your blood" (Hebrews 12:4). The sacrifice of Jesus was on a whole different level—really, in a totally different dimension—than the relatively lightweight troubles we experience such as prejudice and discrimination. We may or may not be called upon to make the ultimate sacrifice, but we should acknowledge that many have and more will be. The crucial point is that we model the Perfecter by actually waging war against the sin nature within us, even to the point of shedding blood if necessary, and becoming dead to sin. This is the path to freedom from sin: our identification with Christ's victory on the cross.

A teenage girl named Sonia offers this poem:

> *Look up, my child, why do you cry?*
>
> *Don't you know that on the cross, for your sins, I died?*

I suffered all the humiliation and pain,

So why do your tears keep falling like rain?

Don't you know that the world could never compare

To the nails through my hands or thorns in my hair?

Look up, my child, don't be blue

The door to salvation is open to you.

Please don't let my works be in vain

Follow me, and in the book, I'll write your name.

The verses in Hebrews 12:5–7 speak words of encouragement, with God addressing us as sons and daughters. Our heavenly Father, like a good earthly father, disciplines us because He loves us, admonishing us to not lose heart when rebuked. We are urged to persevere and run the race, sustaining our relationship with our personal God. This is the great link between square one—God—and resisting sin to the point of death: our crucifixion of sin *in* and through Christ on the cross.

Redemption does not exist outside of Christ. You see, we have no shot at the cure if we do not *individually* acknowledge the Maker of the universe and His power of creation. If we do not accept, by faith, the *original sin of Adam,* it renders everything henceforth meaningless.

As believers, our identity is firmly founded in God, the great I AM, in and through His Son, Jesus Christ. Our core sin is questioning this identity, thus toting around the nature of the first Adam. And the same was true for Moses when he questioned himself ("Who am *I*?") and questioned God ("Who are *You*?"). So the act of questioning our identity in Christ is our sin (singular), which paves the way for sins (plural).

Identity is the key. We are identified with Christ on the cross: dying to sin, dying to ourselves, dying to the nature of Adam. Jesus came and died to become everything we *are* so that we can become everything He *is*!

This should give us such freedom and joy to walk in forgiveness. We must step back and realize that when we sin it is covered, it is finished. Why? How? Because of the amazing love of I AM. God became man to take on our sin. Jesus died once, for everyone. He died in the past for our present and future sins. And He rose from the dead so that each of us can live *in* Him if only we choose to do so. "He Himself bore our sins in his body on the tree, so that we might die to sins and live for righteousness, by his wounds you have been healed" (1 Peter 2:24). This is why God sent His Son, and this is why we are already covered.

This is the perspective, the identity, with which we must regard ourselves because God sees us this way: *We are in Christ.* We have freedom from all sin because of who *we are* in Christ! More than just sharing His sufferings, this allows us the opportunity to *fellowship in* His sufferings—truly *with* Him. If we can grasp this, we can begin to view ourselves as the Lord does: as precious children worthy of the utmost sacrifice. Not just any sacrifice, but the ultimate sacrifice. God becoming man. Taking the sin of the world upon Himself so that we can live free from the bondage of the enemy and inherit eternal life.

Under the Old Covenant, man had to make animal sacrifices to God to atone for sin. The animal had to be spotless. It was a substitute—a literal sacrifice to God to cover the sins of man.

But then...enter the Lamb of God. This tedious process of animal sacrifice was rendered completely useless, abolished under the New

Covenant in and through the ultimate, final sacrifice of Jesus Christ! Blameless, spotless before God the Father. To atone for our sin, once and for all. To bridge the separation from God which man chose to create.

One and done.

The redemptive work *was* done, and *is* done on the cross at Calvary. Think about it. This is life-changing information. God sent His only Son to die on our behalf *because of our mistakes.* An unblemished substitute for our sin. One perfect sacrifice prepared by God, for us.

It's amazing grace. He made this decision because He loves us *that* much.

Grasp this, and you can begin to comprehend how sin is defeated, how we are forgiven, and how we are able to live in daily freedom in Christ!

> *I grew up seriously confused about my sexuality and lived most of my life in and out of homosexuality. Until one day I finally built up the courage, through desperation, to surrender everything over to God. Confess my sins and ask Him to cleanse me of the burden of homosexuality. Through faith, the daily renewing of my mind through God's Word, and by claiming the truth of God's Word for myself, I have been set free from homosexuality. The Word of God says that when we accept Jesus as Lord and Savior and are baptized in Christ we become a "new creation"—the old self is crucified, done away with. My old homosexual lifestyle has been crucified with Christ! I have been "washed, sanctified, and justified through Christ Jesus" and am given "power and authority to ... defeat all the power of the enemy." These truths I now claim for myself and walk in the victory of Christ.*

Jesus Christ did not merely die *for* us, He died *as* us. This is why there is no sin that is greater than God and His forgiveness. This is why *it is finished*.

Jesus is not only the gate to heaven after we die, but Jesus is also the gate to abundant life here and now. That's Good News! That's the Gospel!

We become what we behold. Behold Christ and you'll become more and more like Him. Seek the face of God and you'll see yourself *in* Him!

Claim your new, powerful identity. Live it with confidence. After all, God became man and made the ultimate sacrifice so you would know who you really are.

You're His, a child of God. And He's yours, your Savior and Lord, the perfecter of your faith.

Let's live like it.

CHAPTER ELEVEN

At His Feet

Beware the barrenness of a busy life.
— Socrates

So what does it mean to "behold God?" How do we do that? How do we truly abide in Him so that our identity is firmly rooted in Christ?

As I contemplate these questions, I am reminded of the examples of three women: Mildred, Martha, and Mary.

Recently, my Aunt Mildred suffered a brain hemorrhage. Her symptoms from this trauma were similar to those of a stroke. She lost all ability to move her body, to walk, and even to talk. Aunt Mildred had to learn how to speak and even to walk all over again, much like a small child. But just three months after the hemorrhage, we took her to lunch, and she was able to talk plainly about her remarkable recovery.

When asked how she did it, she would say, "I have no idea. Only God."

Abiding, trusting in the Lord.

In a different but not-so-recent story, Martha invited Jesus and His followers into her house and went to prepare a meal. While working hard in the kitchen, she fumed that her sister Mary was sitting at Jesus' feet and neglecting the work. Martha grew resentful, so she complained to Jesus that she was overworking and asked Him to tell

Mary to help her. But Jesus knew that Martha was drawing attention to herself. Here she was in a different room, saying, "But look at me, look at all the work I'm doing! What about me?" So Jesus praised Mary for spending her time and energy where she should be ... with the son of God (see Luke 10:38–42).

There are countless activities and concerns vying for our attention. Each day we devote huge chunks of our time, thought, and energy to these tasks and efforts. But what would happen if, like Aunt Mildred, you were not able to devote your time, thought, and energy to anything whatsoever? Where would your mind be, what would your hands do, what would your lips say...if you literally had no conscious control? Would your Godly character and identity in Christ take over?

In the hospital, Mildred's first words—and only words for days— were, "God is faithful...God is so good." Though she was disoriented and could not articulate, the praise of God was still on her lips as she spoke of God's faithfulness. The extraordinary thing is that Mildred really had no idea what she was saying. She was not cognizant enough to consciously recall and quote Scripture. In her stroke-like state, she brought Jesus' insight to life: "The things that come out of a person's mouth come from the heart" (Matthew 15:18). Her joyful, trust-filled utterances came as a *natural* overflow of a heart open and surrendered to her living God!

Jesus said in Luke 6:45, "A good man brings good things out of the good stored up in his heart ... For the mouth speaks what the heart is full of." Not only did the Lord honor this woman's faithfulness by so quickly healing and restoring her, He also continued to use her as a direct messenger through those obedient and expectant lips as she asked doctors and nurses alike, "Do you know Jesus?" Mildred was totally like a child at this point, with a beautiful childlike faith. No wonder the Lord chose to use her and heal her! Like a child, she had no doubt that her heavenly Father would take care of her.

We can only speculate what was going in the mind of my Aunt Mildred after this trauma to her brain. But she was never out of touch with her heavenly Father. She was *in* Christ, identity-branded, marked by the Lord Himself. Her body was in a hospital room within the intensive care unit, but her spirit was sitting at the feet of Jesus, soaking up His presence.

Something about Mary

Abiding in Christ. It's easier said than done, but in the story from Luke, Mary gives us the perfect example.

She submits to Jesus, sitting before Him.

She looks only to Him, seeking His face.

She listens to Him, speaking not a word.

Soaking, basking in the presence of Jesus Himself.

Have you been there? Have you ever experienced this? Even a glimpse?

If you have, the evidence will be a *relationship* like the one Mary illustrates—not busyness, religion, works, or service, as Martha illustrates.

Mary sought Jesus' face. She abided in Him.

We must come to the bottom of ourselves, emptying ourselves to Him. We must reach past the busyness of service, past the pews of the church, to a personal yearning for the moment-by-moment filling of God.

What else is necessary, really, when we focus on seeking His face? Like Mary at the feet of Jesus, like a child, soaking up the words and goodness of Jesus…when we seek His face, everything else— *everything* else—falls by the wayside.

In His presence, we can see visions.

In His presence, we can see the reality of our dreams in His will.

In His presence, we can sort the wheat from the chaff.

In His presence, we can gain the confidence and strength to actually do the utmost things we are called to do.

In His presence, there is forgiveness. We rid ourselves of pride, callousness, cynicism, worry, and doubt.

In His presence, there is no fear. Only freedom.

Can you imagine how we would live if we truly walked in this spirit?

Can you imagine what we could do in the name and power of Christ, if we truly abide in His presence?

The Marthazation of Society

Our society is so obsessed with being busy that we have a tendency to correlate busyness with productivity—even with success. This, of course, is a recipe for disaster when this mindset spills over into the church or Christian service. Martha fell prey to busyness and resentfulness rather than choosing to honor Jesus by simply enjoying His presence. Yet Jesus commended Mary, who sat at His feet, making the priority to spend time with Him in genuine fellowship.

Jesus probably knew that Martha was seeking recognition from Him for her hard work and service, but He warned against the "works" running ahead of the "relationship." No matter how eager and capable and hard working we are, we cannot earn or purchase a close relationship with Jesus. Instead, He tells us to keep our focus on the intimate relationship with Him.

Jesus didn't ask Mary to run into the kitchen to whip up more food, or have her grab more flowers for the dining room table. Why? Because He was spending quality time with Mary, in true relationship.

The point at which some Christians, in their effort to "serve" Christ, run ahead of their energy supply is the syndrome called "Marthazation."

> *No matter how busy a man is, he is never too busy to stop and talk about how busy he is.*
>
> — *Kahlil Gibran*

Christians worldwide report that they are, in effect, too busy for God. In data collected from more than twenty thousand Christians with ages ranging from fifteen to eighty-eight, across 139 countries, the "Obstacles to Growth" survey found that on average, six in ten Christians say that it's "often" or "always" true that "the busyness of life gets in the way of developing my relationship with God."

By profession, pastors were most likely to say they rush from task to task (54 percent), which also gets in the way of developing their personal relationship with God (65 percent). "It's tragic. And ironic. The very people who could best help us escape the bondage of busyness are themselves in chains," said Dr. Michael Zigarelli, who conducted the study.

While the study does not explain *why* Christians are so busy and distracted, Zigarelli described the problem among Christians as "a vicious cycle" prompted by cultural conformity: "The accelerated pace and activity level of the modern day distracts us from God and separates us from the abundant, joyful, victorious life He desires for us."

> *They're too busy trying to save everyone else's souls but their own.*
>
> — *Study respondent*

No individual, no leader, no matter how noble in intent, is immune to the lure of Performance Christianity. This *human* power source is severely limited and leads directly to burnout. Too many Christians seem to operate more on their own need than on Christ's love. Most selfishly, and perhaps to ease our conscience, we are really thinking, "I need to convert you to feel good about myself in order to continue to be inspired."

God is not merely inspiration. God is the source of power, and our relationship with Him is paramount. If we do not take time to abide in the relationship, we will run ahead of God. Marthazation, you see, is a problem of displaced service, which can be traced to displaced identity. If we can grasp that our identity is firmly rooted *in Christ*, then we are linked with the energy supply line—God Himself.

Where Is the Hunger?

> *For the past fifteen years, I've been a worker in the church, serving on committees, but plagued with secret doubts about my salvation. I've prayed for God to show me if I had really become His child. My friend, who is a counselor, invited me to talk about what was bothering me. She questioned me until I yelled at her that I questioned the existence of God. After more questions, we agreed that I didn't question God's existence; I questioned whether God existed in my own life. I could believe that Jesus came to save the world's sins, but I didn't believe that He came to save ME from MINE. That night I trusted Him as MY Savior and now I KNOW THAT I KNOW HE IS IN MY LIFE.*

Do you remember the first time you "knew that you knew" God is real? It may have been the day of your salvation. It may have been at an extraordinary event around which you truly felt His presence, or during a particularly meaningful service or personal prayer time. Like the wind, we cannot see it, but we certainly feel the effect of the Spirit—subtle yet powerful.

Because we have seen a glimpse of His power and presence, we know when we are *not* in union and fellowship with our God. We yearn, as this Keith Green lyric desperately depicts, to draw ourselves back into right relationship with the Lord:

My eyes are dry

My faith is old

My heart is hard

My prayers are cold

But I know how I ought to be,

Alive to you, and dead to me.

Aren't we over ourselves yet?

Aren't we tired of chasing our own dreams instead of living *His* plan?

Aren't we weary of focusing so much on our phones, our gadgets, our agenda, our day, our schedule, our concerns, our fears, and ourselves?

Personally, I am. I'm worn out. I'm tired of living a life that reflects conditional love for Christ, who gave it all for us. I'm weary of a commitment seemingly based more on whims, inspirations, circumstances, and feelings rather than on an unconditional commitment modeled for us and required of us.

I'm burdened ... and I want to just thrust it off and find out, really, what this living for Jesus is all about.

> *Do nothing out of selfish ambition or vain conceit, but in humility consider others better than yourselves.*
>
> — *Philippians 2:3*

Where Is the Love?

I'm a normal teenager; I have a mom and a dad whom I love with all my heart. All my life I have known God and always believed in Him, but I didn't really "know Him" until I went to camp. It was there that I fell in love with Jesus Christ. Believe me, it was the best thing in the world! All my life I was looking for that one missing piece that would make my life complete, and it was Jesus Christ. I found the missing part of my life.

But as many of us do, I lost connection with Him because of school and friends and I didn't even realize that every day we don't pray, our relationship grows farther and farther apart until we're at the point where we have to start at square one.

The Lord brought me to that point. And God led me to a new school where He is in my life again. My relationship with Jesus is renewed and I found Christ once again. I found a youth group and Bible study group and I'm a strong Christian. I'm happy and I'm loved by many. Praise the Lord!

Where is the love, the first-fruit of my relationship with God? The love for Christ that comes unadulterated from my heart to His—not because of what He has done for me, but because of *who He is*.

God cannot do anything more than He has already done to make us love Him or adore Him more than we already do. We simply love Him because of who He is. Likewise, you and I cannot do one thing to make Him love us any more or less than He already does. *This* is great news! When we begin to punch into this frame of mind, we're set free. We realize that service and works draw God exactly zero inches closer to our hearts than He already is.

All because our identity is finished *in* and *with* Christ.

Furthermore, all the good that we want to do, all the noble service that we may desire to offer up to the Lord—all of it—can never increase His love for us. He loves us for *who* we are because we are *in* Him! Period.

For I am convinced that neither death nor life, neither angels nor demons, neither the present nor the future, nor any powers, neither height nor depth, nor anything else in all creation, will be able to separate us from the love of God that is in Christ Jesus our Lord.

— *Romans 8:38, 39*

As the camp director told Eli in the story in Chapter One, "You can't act right, dress right, and smell right *enough* to make Him love you one ounce more than He already does. He just loves you. He just *loves* you."

We have this earnest and sincere desire to be "used" by God. This is all well and good. But check your desire: Is it truly for Him and His purposes? Or is it so that we can feel useful, in a modern-day sense, or so that we can have a tangible record of what we have accomplished for Him?

Are we devoted to Christ, or just busy?

Like a person considering retirement, when we look this issue straight in the eyes, who are we without our work? Take away our daily tasks, goals, and accomplishments … and who are we, really, when we have no résumé to speak of? But isn't this the way the Lord wants us? Remember Moses, the humble sheepherder, who was extracted from forty years in the wilderness. Who was he? Far from a prince. And this is the point at which God might see fit to use us if it so pleases Him. Stripped of busyness, of credentials, of résumés and pedigrees. Just us … abiding and willing.

I have to admit, this notion was quite an impediment for me in writing this book. I could not properly write it until I took the journey myself. A journey not yet completed, mind you, but one merely embarked upon.

I passionately believe that this work is the calling of my life, and that it had to be written and shared. But is it my work for God, or is it just lip service so that I could feel my efforts were *useful*? If it were never written, published, and shared, what would my training and research all have been for? It wouldn't have been validated in the eyes of others or myself. I had to self-examine, re-direct, and surrender the entire project to the Lord.

After almost twenty years of thought, work, and devotion, you are reading the product of that journey. The fresh discoveries, epiphanies, and conclusions along the way are too many to count. But I realized that the project was bigger than I was. So I gave it up. I willfully placed the book in His hands—and He took it and gave it the life He intended for it to have.

Like the calling of Moses, and like almost any calling we feel, my calling was actually a disruption. A disruption inevitably changes our direction from our own preconceived plan. But, as promised in accordance with a calling, God has been with me. Had I not taken time to sit at His feet, I know for certain that this project wouldn't have been worth sharing with others. Had I failed to abide in Him, sure enough, it would have been for my sake and not His. More than I could have imagined, and far more than my faith expected, He has met and guided me at every session, every chapter, every page, every line…and, I trust, at every thought as well.

And in this way, as Moses sheepishly gave in to His calling, I had no choice but to give in to mine, and place my faith in God's timing.

Where Is the Commitment?

Everyone who's ever taken a shower has an idea. It's the person who gets out of the shower, dries off, and does something about it who makes the difference.

—— *John Maxwell*

I have every confidence that our Lord will meet you in your place of surrender with an undeniable calling that just won't let go until you answer it. In His timing, in His place.

It is never, ever too late to wake up and answer the call. This godly burden will remain on your shoulders and in your gut— even through the wilderness, even for forty years. The amazing thing is, if it is truly God's call, He *will* equip you to accomplish whatever He calls you to do.

Thankfully, God does not call those who are fit, but He always fits those who are called. If God is calling you to fulfill a role for His purposes, He will meet you where you are, enable you, and empower you. When you marshal the courage to hold up your end of the deal, He will specifically equip you beyond your faith or imagination to accomplish the task. Step out, take action, and your faith will catapult you to higher levels—not because of who you are in yourself, but *because of who you are in Christ.*

This is where we want to be in order to truly help others. At Jesus' feet, abiding in Him. As we do so, we'll be comfortable enough with ourselves that we can simply get out of the way and serve others by pointing them to Christ.

Isaiah 52:2 urges us, "Shake off your dust; rise up ... Free yourself from the chains on your neck." We must shake off the dust that our post-Christian culture has subtly cast upon us. The modern fascination with so-called tolerance has led to a lack of absolutes and, inevitably, to a general disobedience to God. Many Christians find themselves buried in the dust of fear, intimidation, and apathy. We've become numb to the Spirit within us. Dust is nothing but dirt. Much like silver place settings tucked away in a cabinet, we've become tarnished due to lack of use.

Experts estimate that 97 percent of Christians operate in a comfort zone, and only 3 percent operate in an active-effective zone. Let's be part of that 3 percent. Active. Effective. Not in our own strength and effort, but because we are so steeped in the love of Jesus Christ that we cannot help seeing the needs around us and meeting those needs with love.

Gretchen's story illustrates how we must often challenge ourselves, consciously and deliberately, to stretch, grow, and shine:

> I've been praying, and God is changing my "tight-wadness"(sic) in small ways. It began with a God-given idea: I now try to carry one-dollar bills with me, and whenever I'm in a public restroom, I tip the lady who is there with her cleaning cart. It is a very small act, but for me, it is practicing spontaneous generosity and is doable.

This Good Samaritan didn't step in front of a train, or swim a mile in a hurricane to save a drowning child. She merely acted, because her abiding relationship with Jesus would not allow her to *not* act. She felt something and then did something. It was small, but effective.

God isn't necessarily looking for the spectacular. There is genuine beauty in average, ordinary obedience. So stop coasting. Don't fall for Marthazation and be busy for busy's sake, but start at the feet of Jesus. As you rest and abide in Him, you'll find that He invigorates you for what's truly important.

On the other hand, be cautious of the desire to be used by God for the sake of service or self-fulfillment. Abide at His feet, love Him, listen to His voice, and pray to be used naturally to help others—in His way, in His time.

Love God. Abide in Christ. Without plans, preconceptions, or pretense. The rest will surely follow.

CHAPTER TWELVE

It's About Others

We do not exist for ourselves alone, and it is only when we are fully convinced of this fact that we begin to love ourselves properly and thus also love others. What do I mean by loving ourselves properly? I mean, first of all, desiring to live, accepting life as a very great gift and a great good, not because of what it gives us, but because of what it enables us to give to others.

— *Thomas Merton*

Joe Kordick was an executive vice-president with Ford Motor Company and on the short list to become president of the company. But everything changed after a missionary from Taiwan stayed at his house and talked about preaching the gospel to remote tribal people.

Kordick responded, "You have a great life. I wish I could do what you are doing."

The missionary replied with a strange question: "How many people do you see on an average day with whom you can spend more than just a passing moment, talking about the things of life?" Kordick thought a moment and said, "I see a hundred people a day that I potentially might speak with."

The missionary responded: "Let me get this straight. In one week you can have five hundred conversations with people? In one week I see maybe twelve people—and only three speak my dialect! Tell me, who is in the right job?"

Then Joe's guest turned the screws. "Your problem is that you are unwilling to surrender to Jesus to let Him lead you in your everyday life to love and care for the people around you."

Kordick was convicted. He had been ignoring Jesus and ignoring others—just furthering his career, serving his own interests. He repented and began intentionally looking for ways to honor Christ and show concern for others by caring enough to speak with them about Jesus. He became known for his spiritual connection with customers.

Then one day he heard Jesus say, *Follow me*. And it wasn't to the presidency of Ford Motor Company. The Lord led Kordick, at age fifty-seven, to give up a $20 million future for a move to Florida to change bedpans as a volunteer with Hospice. Kordick has reflected that ministering at the bedsides of those near death was the most rewarding work of his life.

Paul writes in Acts 20:19, "It is better to give than to receive. I was among you with humility and tears." This is sharing life: knowing people, walking among the needy, protecting and providing for the church of God—not for gain, but to bring them Jesus.

Take it from Mylon LeFevre, a man who achieved tremendous success in the music industry. Born into a gospel-singing family, Mylon began writing songs as a teenager. When he was seventeen years old, his family performed his first song, "Without Him," at a gospel music show. Afterward, a member of the audience asked to meet Mylon. That person was Elvis Presley, who later recorded the song. Over the next year, more than a hundred artists recorded Mylon's songs. At age nineteen, he recorded his first album and went on to sell millions of records. But his journey into the world of rock 'n' roll propelled him into an emotional tailspin. Where Mylon landed after all the hoopla is a place we know exists, and is absolutely for real. The lyrics to his song "More of Jesus" illustrate both his journey and his landing place.

Break my heart and change my mind

Cut me loose from ties that bind

Lead me as I follow you

Give me strength to follow through

Oh, more ... more

I want to be more like Jesus ...

More of Jesus, less of me...

From where does this type of extraordinary commitment come? Is it one's background, personality type, or the drive of a unique person that creates this passion to serve others? How do we tap into this tenderness, this humble attitude of servanthood? Joe Kordick's missionary friend zeroed in on the key ingredient: *surrender.*

Surrendering to Christ means not only staying in touch with the power source, but also daily relinquishing to the Lord the control of our lives. We must *self-surrender* to God—this is true discipleship. It means connecting with people in the midst of their concerns, serving *with* people instead of serving *to* people. Without surrendering, we lose touch with the power and everything falls back to our own strength and effort. Without daily surrender, we lose our identification *with* and *in* Christ, increasingly relying on our own devices. And you know what? That's futile. That's what brings on hypocrisy.

Surrender = Strength

Daily surrendering our lives to Christ, as the missionary challenged Kordick to do, is crucial for each of us because it is at the heart of true communion with our Lord. Many folks seem to have this backwards; we tend to give service higher priority than personal devotion. The inability to separate service from surrender—and the inflexibility to correctly prioritize the two—is an ongoing temptation in Christian circles and among the most practical pitfalls within the church.

Obviously, there is a time and a place for work and service. However, according to Jesus, sitting at His feet was exactly the right place for Mary. Although Jesus and the others were likely very hungry, busy Martha learned that submitting to Jesus—being with Him and spending time with Him—is more important than other people, and even more important than hunger. Why? Because He is the source from which everything else flows. What we learn from the story of Mary and Martha is that surrender is not for rookies. It is not conditional and it is not circumstantial. Surrender is foundational to identification with Christ and is the real gateway to this deep relationship called communion.

If we can muster the courage to turn 180 degrees from society and its humanistic thinking, we'll find that spending time with Jesus—surrendered at His feet, as God intended—is really the foundation from which we do all things well.

Sitting with and submitting to Jesus gives us strength.

Listening to and resting in Jesus infuses us with vigor.

Everything we think, do, and say springs from this relationship. So a heart truly surrendered to Christ quite naturally reflects the One who has unlocked the door to this freedom.

The missionary also spoke to Kordick about "sharing life." Most of us would probably regard the missionary's comment as an obligation— yet another "service." And this is precisely the humanistic, service-oriented mindset that we must surrender. Grasping this fundamental challenge of the Christian life, and putting it into practice with abandonment, is the path to real freedom. Everything lives, breathes, and grows from this base of identification and surrender.

As the story of Joe Kordick radically illustrates, such a personal relationship with Christ springs naturally into public words and deeds of grace, service, and love. The difference between Kordick and others who have heard the challenge is that Kordick took *action*.

Bob Bowman, coach of Michael Phelps, the record-setting athlete who has won the most medals in the history of the Olympic Games, says: "Successful people make a habit of doing things that unsuccessful people don't like to do. That's it. They make a habit of doing things other people aren't willing to do."

Phelps took action. Kordick took action. Action requires total surrender—self-surrender. Just as the Scriptures challenge us to walk at all times in an attitude of prayer, surrender to the Holy Spirit is a mindset that pervades our persona. It is an outlook that goes before us and behind us, and surrounds us as a hedge of grace and protection.

Communion Fosters Communication

The Latin word for communication means "to share." It is the attitude of self-surrender that allows us to take our intimate communion with

God, the deepest form of communication, and share it with others—accurately, truthfully, and in a spirit of empathy and love.

And when we look at sharing the Greatest Story through the lens of identification in Christ, our thinking is turned to God's perspective. To *His* sacrifice. In this spirit, pride and reluctance slough off like dead skin. We have seen the negative effects of stereotyping, and it's time we begin turning the tide by planting positive images and representations, allowing the positive cycle to echo to the ends of the earth. It's also time that we speak. If we don't tell our story, others will tell it for us, and most will get it wrong.

> *"The single biggest problem in communication is the illusion that it has taken place."*
>
> — *George Bernard Shaw*

A point of clarification is in order here. When we talk about building a solid identity in Christ, we're not talking about self-worship. More Christians need to love themselves enough to reach a point in their relationship with Christ where they can conversationally share Him with others. When we're at peace with ourselves, and sitting at the feet of Jesus, we will shine by osmosis—comfortably sharing the message. Gretchen learned this as a result of acting upon her convictions:

> *I'm convinced that in most areas of my life, I cannot make big, overnight changes. Unfortunately, I am stuck in myself, but when I take small steps and do what is doable, God sees my pitiful attempts and mysteriously transforms my soul.*
>
> *And so it is with evangelism and sharing Jesus. I can only do what is doable. I can only take small steps. Sometimes it means praying silently behind someone's back. Sometimes it involves easy chitchat or doing a small act of kindness. But as I continue in these tiny steps, God does His part in creating situations and conversations in which I*

can talk about His Son. Plus, all the doable small steps are increasing my confidence.

I still stumble with words, but sharing Jesus is getting easier and more natural.

So it is only through his rapport with Christ, and the resulting comfort with ourselves, that we are able to even entertain the notion of losing inhibition, of getting the heck out of the way and pointing people to Christ. Seeking Christ first leads to placing Him in front of everything else, and thus placing others before ourselves. After all, Jesus told us to feed His lambs first, not to be *fed* first (see John 21:15).

No Pressure

At the same time, this doesn't mean that one needs to be solid as a rock in order to witness. If we wait on that, we might never speak! As Zechariah 4:6 reminds us, it is not by our might, nor by our power, "but 'by my Spirit,' says the LORD." In *His* Spirit, we are literally His mouthpiece. There is no pressure on us because the Spirit is at work on our behalf. When we are Spirit-directed instead of self-directed, we can listen empathically, realizing that we don't have to save them. That's the Holy Spirit's job. Our job is to love them and to point them to Jesus.

It's about Him, not us.

With this perspective in mind, it's not just a duty to share Christ and not just an obligation. It's not something to be contrived, stressed over, or scripted. *It's an opportunity to share life.* People want relationship. They can intuitively sense the real and the genuine, and that is precisely what they're looking for. It is simply *our story* that others want to hear, free of well intended sermonizing or cajoling.

But we must be real and vulnerable when telling our story, for it is through our weakness that others will clearly see the strength of God. People want to see faith in us. They want to see and hear evidence of things not proven—not a fabricated perfect faith, but an authentic rubber-meets-the-road working faith, by which we daily take up our cross to follow Jesus.

In this spirit, it is a privilege and honor to share how we are identified with and in Jesus Christ. The spotlight is exactly where it should be— off of us, and on Jesus. This is all we are called to do in sharing Him: Just point the way.

Many say we need a fresh dialogue. Folks, Jesus *is* the dialogue. It is our communion with Him which naturally reflects and directs others to Christ. From a dynamic personal faith flows a dynamic public witness. All we need is a new perspective, a fresh dialogue in our personal walk with Him that cannot help but overflow to others— maybe even in the form of a dollar bill to the bathroom custodian.

Jesus is the same yesterday, today, and forever. He is the great I AM. And by the way, that's in the present tense.

His message is in the present tense as well. The message is unchanging, but often our misguided mindset or methodologies need pruning. Collective change begins with personal reformation within each of us, one heart at a time, daily surrendering as living sacrifices to Him: "Do not conform any longer to the pattern of this world, but be transformed by the renewing of your mind" (Romans 12:2).

We learn from Mary that everything, including our witness, begins at the feet of Jesus. The Lord wants us to know Him so intimately that we can present Him to others and describe Him from personal experience—from having seen Him, from having heard His voice, from having felt His touch.

This is the sequence: communion leads to communication. From a profoundly personal relationship with Christ flows a naturally genuine witness. Our communion *in* Christ leads to sincere and effective communication *of* Christ with others.

Communion must come first. Communication follows from this wellspring of life within us.

Jesus the Communicator

Then comes *how* we communicate the incredibly wonderful news of the gospel. To keep a secret is to hold something that others hunger for. People crave the unknown. We are enticed by novels and movies of mystery. We long to see the unseen, hear the unspoken, experience what no one else has experienced. So why lead with the answers? No story ever leads off with the ending. Who would watch? Who would listen?

Jesus was a master communicator. Did you know that the Gospels record 153 questions Jesus asked His listeners? He used visual and sensory communication including the rites of communion, baptism, and the laying on of hands. And He was also a storyteller. Almost half of His words in Matthew, and over half of His words in Luke, are parables (Lewis & Lewis, 1989). He often spoke to crowds of thousands, but never once used a microphone. People walked for miles in their sandals and bare feet solely to hear His words.

Jesus is our incarnate example of the Christian message. This is *contextual incarnation*. And Jesus lived it out in practical terms. He came to us, met us where we live, and communicated on our level.

He spoke in context, using relevant metaphors and vivid similes. He spoke the vernacular of common people by speaking to fishermen about catching fish, to tax collectors about money, and to herdsmen and farmers about the land and soil.

C.S. Lewis said, "It is absolutely disgraceful that we expect missionaries to the Bantus to learn Bantu but never ask whether our missionaries to the Americans or English can speak American or English." Lewis was saying that good communication takes place at the hearer's level—how he speaks and thinks, where he lives, what he relates to—and not at the communicator's level. So are we really speaking the language of the recipient?

We need not look any further than the Scriptures as the beginning and end of how to conduct our lives, how to identify with others, and how to share its inherent message. In order to connect with others, pay attention to *how* the Bible communicates as well as to *what* it communicates. Watch the author of Job being asked the most vexing philosophical question we face: why do bad things happen to good people? Listen to Solomon teach his son how to honor God and be a success in God's world. Solomon feeds his son short sentences that are long remembered. If we will pay attention to form as well as content— to *how* God communicates as well as *what* He communicates—all the variety we need for connecting to American "Bantus" is found in the text itself.

Jesus often began a teaching point by saying, in effect, "Once upon a time...." Again, the master communicator uses narrative. Jesus was sent to the Bantus of earth. He not only understood the language and tradition and lifestyle of His audience, He also cared to understand where people were coming from. He embodied empathy. He found common ground from which to relate. Using word pictures and open dialogue, Jesus came to meet us exactly where we are. Jesus is our ultimate example of how to effectively contextualize the message.

In Matthew 9:9–13 we see how Jesus—God in the flesh— freely associates with secular culture. To Matthew, a tax collector, He says, "Follow me." Immediately Matthew drops what he's doing and goes with Jesus. Jesus is invited to His new disciple's home for dinner. There, Matthew's tax-collector friends join them. Creating relationship and communion with one led to natural rapport with others.

Jesus showed no reluctance or reservation about sharing a meal with unbelievers. These people broke bread together with the Bread of Life. As respect and trust grew, barriers fell. Therein lies the power of vulnerability: we allow the Holy Spirit to do His work as we share. We see in this passage how Christ was inextricably linked with His source. We can almost envision Him walking and talking as though driven by the source, drawing in power with each breath like oxygen.

As in many other instances in the Gospels, the major obstacles to Jesus' ministry at Matthew's table were the religious leaders themselves. Thinking they had "caught" Him in a compromising position, the Pharisees spread word that Christ was dining with tax collectors and "sinners." When the objections and questions reached Jesus, He declared: "It is not the healthy who need a doctor, but the sick. But go and learn what this means: 'I desire mercy, not sacrifice.' For I have not come to call the righteous, but sinners to repentance" (Matthew 9:12–13).

Jesus is the Word. Jesus, the Word, sits and eats and fellowships with tax collectors and "sinners." The Word is *in* us and with us when we follow His example and do the same.

Contagious Christianity

> *The reality is that in this life, we never arrive, but in the next, we will get to see the evidence of all of what we have lived and become through Christ. We will see how much we achieved and how much more we could've achieved.*
>
> *We have a choice. We can keep God to ourselves or we can share Him. It is really very simple. Sharing Him is frightening, sometimes terrifying, and often we find ways to avoid it.*

This person's words remind us that, like Moses, even though the calling or task may be daunting, we can move forward with confidence in humility. Without compromising, we can find ourselves unafraid of and unthreatened by secular culture.

Why? Our identity in Jesus Christ. Jesus was clear about His identity ("For I have not come to call the righteous, but sinners to repentance"). You and I should be equally as clear about our identities. We are *in* Christ. He is *in* us. We are children of the King of Kings because He took our sin upon Himself and adopted us into His family. This is true today, tomorrow, and forever.

We have received Him and are called righteous. Not because we're special, but because our sin was imparted directly to Him. He became sin for us. He came to sacrifice Himself for all sinners, calling them and drawing them unto Himself. With this knowledge and spiritual realization, how then can we even think of concealing such an escape from bondage? As Christ modeled and identified with us, so we are to model and identify with others.

One of my South Korean friends, for whom English is a second language, had an interesting way of putting it. He once said, "We want to contaminate other people with our enthusiasm so they too will want what we have." Well, he almost nailed it. What we want is for what we have in Christ to be *contagious*. This doesn't mean that we inject or force our beliefs—or contaminate people—it means that we introduce and model the difference that Jesus makes. This is what allows the Holy Spirit to do the real work.

"All the Damn Christians"

CHAPTER THIRTEEN

Turning Hypocrisy into Opportunity

The world can no longer be left to mere diplomats, politicians, and
business leaders. They have done the best they could, no doubt.
But this is an age for spiritual heroes—a time for men and women
to be heroic in their faith and in spiritual character and power.
The greatest danger to the Christian church today is
that of pitching its message too low.

— *Dallas Willard*

When asked to state the gospel (Christian message) the way they understand it to be, four professing Christians gave these responses:

> *I wish I knew. I have been trying to put everything together. It is embarrassing to me that I don't know. I want to learn more. I believe in God. I just don't know why or how.*

> *I've heard the message so many times that I wouldn't know where to start.*

> *Three words: Just be good.*

> *I was raised as a Christian. I have some doubts about what exactly I believe, but I am concrete on Jesus being the Son of God and my Savior.*

Christianity is a faith of transcendence. However, when placed in the arena of life, many Christians fail to act in ways that offer much of a glimpse of transcendence. In fact, one of the conclusions from our study is that not enough professing Christians actually understand what they believe. Our audience hears our promises of a transcendent life and expects to see something different. But because we often aren't sure what we believe, we have little idea how to act in a way that meets their expectations.

Hypocritical? Who's to blame here, anyway? How can we improve the situation?

It seems complicated—a conundrum that cannot be easily rectified. But just as we have with the message itself, we the followers of Christ— the Pharisees, the hypocrites, the sinners—have personally blurred the view of those outside of our insulated subculture. Consequently, non-believers are largely rejecting a gospel that has been only half-told, a counterfeit message mispresented or misrepresented by many of us who call ourselves Christians.

Too often, as outsiders look inside our camp, one glimpse is all they need to keep searching elsewhere. We absolutely cannot allow this to continue—the world's rejection of Christianity due to our human misrepresentation of the faith. The good news of Jesus Christ is entrusted to us to represent accurately, fully, and confidently, so that folks can clearly see Jesus.

The stories I shared earlier of Donnie and Lillian are tragic: Donnie, a young man eager to learn more about the Lord, was stood up by the pastor who failed to show for dinner, and Lillian, the elderly woman, who was embittered by the preacher (and God) after a humiliating incident in church during her teen years. But the real travesty in these stories is that both Donnie and Lillian allowed flawed human beings to scapegoat the gospel. They threw out the baby with the bath water.

Just as it was directly hypocritical of the pastor and evangelist who gave a golf game higher priority than Donnie's invitation to answer questions over dinner, it was overtly hypocritical of the legalistic preacher who scolded Lillian in front of the whole church. On the other hand, it was shortsighted of Donnie to equate flawed messengers with what Jesus is all about, and shortsighted of Lillian to allow the overzealous accusation of the preacher to distort her view of a loving God who wants to be close to her. After all, what did any of this have to do with the person of Jesus?

And this is part of our own hypocrisy as well: looking the other way while these folks, millions upon millions of them, are allowed to harbor their pain. The pain of lost hope. The pain of betrayal, manifested in cynicism and bitterness.

Unfortunately, we Christian soldiers have left a trail of tears as we marched on.

Redemption in the Message

You may be wondering, where were the authentic Christians in Donnie and Lillian's stories?

I can tell you about one.

He knocked not once, but several times before the old woman answered the door. He saw past her facade when she turned him away. Without coercing, he used his God-given character and friendliness to gain the privilege to enter her home.

They sat together. She talked. He listened.

Though the man was a pastor and she didn't trust him, it was evident that Lillian was a person with a lot on her mind and a weight burdening her heart. She divulged her story for the first time since that day at the altar. Through her tears, she confessed her disappointment and pain, revealing that she had harbored the terrible experience of public humiliation and scorn against the church and against Christians for years and years.

He pointed her to Jesus, the only redeemer of hope—past, present, and future.

It was when she contemplated Jesus that she saw her own hypocrisy. As the visiting pastor offered to pray with her, she forgave the preacher who had scolded her all those years before. And she did something else that only took a few seconds, but was a monumental step. She forgave herself. Decades of festering bitterness, pride, and hurt all faded at the feet of Jesus, simply because the visiting pastor listened and pointed her there. But what was it that brought the pastor to Lillian's home? After all, he knew she was a woman who hadn't darkened the door of a church for over seventy years.

The pastor was there because he had been where Lillian had been, having experienced similar hurt and pain several years before. You see, he was the pastor who had stood up Donnie to finish his round of golf. Despondent and feeling a devastating sense of conviction after Donnie's suicide, this pastor vowed that he would never again pass up an opportunity to point someone, *anyone*, to Jesus.

And that is what drove him to visit Lillian.

Sure, we are a beaten and battered bunch, but there is real redemption in the wondrous message we often represent so tepidly. Truth be told, we should not even have to be reminded of Christ's *command* to share Him with others. The pastor knew firsthand after his costly round of golf that sharing Christ is not an obligation, ritual, or duty— but a *privilege*.

Helping others discover the freedom and everlasting life that we enjoy is an honor. You and I are the hand-chosen representatives of the King of Kings and Lord of Lords, the creator and master of the universe. What a privilege it is to serve Him as His ambassadors, sharing His life-giving salvation and grace with young and old alike. Do we fail to live accordingly? Sure. Do we make mistakes—even well-intended ones? You bet. But as the pastor's own redemption and devotion shows, we are never too old to learn from our mistakes and make mid-course corrections. Getting over ourselves, confessing our failures to God, and walking in the power and guidance of His Holy Spirit could mean an eternal difference in someone's life. Someone like Lillian.

Good News Rules

So we've drudged through the bad news: our mispresentations, misrepresentations, hypocrisy, and the world's cycle of stereotyping. All excuses, really. Scapegoats.

So now, we must confront and learn from our mistakes. What would the point of this book be if we just left it at reporting the alarming and convicting responses about Christianity and Christian hypocrisy? What if the pastor had not changed things up? What if he had continued to be more concerned about drives and putts than lives and hearts?

Where we now must look, and lock in, is on the good news. The powerful nature of our Redeemer, and what He has done for us through the cross, far exceeds and transcends all the junk that impedes us from effectively telling the Greatest Story.

As we heed His invitation to cast all our cares on Him, truth emerges from the fog and we can see and learn from our mistakes. We can begin practicing what we preach by giving our own disappointments, rejections, and failures to Him who has redeemed us. Because of His sacrifice on the cross, it is finished—as it must be if we are to represent the same to others. By excavating the logs from our own eyes, we can see much more clearly the need, the cry, and the facade of others.

Sometimes folks have asked me about my faith in God, and oftentimes argued their case against it—which used to baffle me because their arguments appeared to be based on ignorance. I can't believe in fantasy or some ethereal being out there beyond the blue. I have to have solid evidence and facts to back it up. And, I have to say, I am willing to chase after those facts and research until I am satisfied.

I refuse to allow traditions and rites and denominationalism to stand in my way. I don't take the word of mere "men" to stand in the way of me finding out the truth. It's there, but you have to be prepared to be surprised, challenged, and changed—especially in your views of what you think is acceptable or "norm" (based on previous expectations, teachings, or upbringing).

They always say truth is stranger than fiction. And so it is!

To try to put it into a box and say it is "thus and thus" is folly. No one can put God in a box and never should, either. That's reducing Him down to our level when He is far and above all that.

During all my years of searching and longing for solid ground, I have been the one to change in my thinking and way of seeing things and in my understanding. All the time growing and changing and maturing.

I have solid grounds for my faith and have the personal experiences to back it up, too. If a personal relationship with our creator is worth having, then it's worth pursuing!

I began [my search] as a young girl because I was tired of "dead religion" that got me nowhere and, in fact, bored me silly and sent me to sleep at the back of the church! I complained to God back then that it was all so boring and shouldn't be like that. That is when I started my journey of discovery. I am still traveling along it.

Now I have had another cry of my heart answered, to understand the true translations of His Word, and my thinking has been challenged even more to remove the boxes. Now it is exciting, exhilarating, absorbing, enormous, amazing, and informative beyond my wildest hopes.

It really has blown away the limits previously placed to see all things in a totally new light, and the best thing is, religion has absolutely no part in it.

This is grabbing life at its deepest level.

Now I can see why God hates religion and why He says, "My people perish through lack of knowledge." Truth is worth the changes and the pursuing.

It depends on how much a person really wants it.

One heart, one life at a time. It is this cyclical nature of a person gaining understanding and freedom, and in turn, passing it on to others that will lead to the ultimate goal of having a positive impact on secular culture.

Rules of Engagement

If we don't know God, how can we represent Him? Knowing, understanding, and conveying the message cannot precede knowing the author of the message, who is God Himself. Branded through identification with Christ, we are "agents" for the Lord. We are made in His image to speak for, to mediate for, and to represent Him to others.

How can we relate? How will we connect to others such as this respondent?

> *My parents are Catholic. They forced me to go through Confirmation;*
> *but I'm not ready to pick a religion; also, I'm a gay male, and thus do*
> *not want to participate in religious institutions that preach against*
> *the way I am.*

Like Scripture and the parables, and like the message itself, the answer to how to improve our relationship with others is simple yet profound. We must get back to God before we can effectively learn, relearn, communicate, or re-communicate the message of His Son.

Know Him and worship Him for who He is. I AM. He is the God of history, the God of the present, the God of the future. Love Him, adore Him. He is personal. Greater is He that is in *you* than he that is in the world.

Then follow the practical communication form, methodology, and content of our model. Though He was sent from God and was God in the human form, Christ freely mixed with secular culture. He was the ultimate boundary spanner.

Corporations often hire public relations specialists to act as "boundary spanners" between the corporation and the public. The purpose is to create knowledge of the corporation's products and services, and to make sure the public understands what the company is about. It's a simple concept and not a bad idea at all. Well, the church could use some boundary spanning. And some bridge building wouldn't hurt either. The challenge to Christians is to incorporate these elements of open exchange while going *outside* the church and spanning the often impermeable boundaries. Through cultivation of common ground, the Christian message may be presented uncompromisingly, in the vernacular of the individual or group to whom it is directed. Following the lead of the Holy Spirit, any sincere person can balance the delicate nature of this genuine dialogue. In this way, we follow the example of Jesus by bridging the apparent divide between Christendom and secular culture.

Boundary spanners are those who are girded with truth, rooted in their identity with Christ, and firmly footed with the readiness that comes from the gospel of peace. They flow in the Spirit, which begins and ends at the feet of Jesus. By listening to Him, soaking up His words, and becoming more and more like Him, we naturally develop a concern and empathy to listen to and openly communicate with others. As Paula wrote:

> *I am frequently amazed at the power of listening. I bumped into my neighbor yesterday and hadn't chatted with her in person for a little while. I asked her how things were going with one of her children, and listened. I was awed, amazed, moved, and touched by what she shared.*
>
> *I felt "sacredness."*
>
> *She is in a painful and difficult place with this one child. I was touched by her honesty, her tears, her wondering and questioning. I prayed in my heart for her, that God would somehow draw close to her and help.*
>
> *I reminded myself to simply listen.*

As Paula's story so practically illustrates, relationship building starts with individuals, those closest to us, especially our neighbors. Rather than merely asking the obligatory "How are you?" in passing, Paula took an extra empathic step by asking about a specific concern regarding her neighbor's child. The thoughtfulness to ask about a concern is the first step. Asking it sincerely opens the door for openhearted responses like those given to Paula. People can easily sense whether we are asking a question as a passing greeting or if we are genuinely inquiring as if we want to know and listen to their story.

We are simply opening the door, as Paula did.

Spending time listening to and valuing the opinions and ideas of others creates not only a rapport, but also a foundation of communication and trust from which we can establish and cultivate new relationships. Going through the motions will not cut it. Our audience must *believe* we are truly listening. In this way, the individual approach—one heart at a time—can positively turn the world's pre-conceived images of hypocrisy on our part. Relationships are a privilege, built with effort over time. Cultivated and nurtured. Forged, not forced. Mutually beneficial, not manipulative.

There is simply more expected of those who choose to live by a code or standard. But those who make accusations that we are not living up to that mark must have an inherent understanding, or at least a recognition, of our code. This recognition suggests an element of latent respect, and also establishes that at one point there was the feeling of relationship between what Christianity claims and what humans long for. Many who are not believers do respect the basic tenants of Christianity. In fact, many respondents wrote positively about Christianity. For example:

> *It is a good religion with a lot of great moral foundation.*

> *I (and all Muslims) believe in Jesus and Christianity as well and respect them.*

> *It is a respectable religion that has done many wonderful things for people.*

So the higher ideal and hope of Christianity is often very powerful to those who long for something to believe in. Hypocrisy, mispresentation, and misrepresentation on our part destroy that trust and encourage the protective behavior of cynicism. In this context, cynicism is the mark of a closed mind often resulting from a disappointed heart.

Cynicism may be rampant, but community is universal. Everyone wants it. More importantly, as the story of Derek shows us, everyone *needs* this sense of belonging:

> *I'm going to kill myself, I thought. I was a teenager. My life consisted of school, hate, pornography, and video games. I felt betrayed by my friends and family, as if they had always been against me. At age twelve, I felt I was not too young to die. Nobody noticed me, nobody talked to me. I felt nobody cared for me.*
>
> *My life was such a confusing mess.*
>
> *All I wanted was care and compassion from other people.*
>
> *One day my sister invited me to go to church. The people were so friendly. It felt like a family. I wanted to know their secret. At a summer camp, the speaker told me how he had found Jesus. He told how Jesus died for him and for each of us. He explained how Jesus was like his best friend, and that he felt really free for the first time in his life. He said that if we invited Jesus into our lives, we too could feel free. He was right. I am now free and not lonely any more.*

The feeling of community begins through communion with our Lord. This fosters positive and sincere two-way communication with the people He places in our path. And when they do cross our path, how may we practically address spiritual things and share life with them?

Points of Contact with Secular Culture

> *I have become all things to all people so that by all possible means I might save some.*
>
> — *1 Corinthians 9:22*

Because of dogmatic or antagonistic presenters of the Christian message, stereotypes have been formed among non-believers that all Christians, and in fact the Christian faith, are dogmatic and antagonistic. This, of course, further diminishes openness and understanding, which makes our task tougher. When asked how the recollected message he heard could be improved, one respondent said:

> *If the preacher had been more loving. When people are "bullied" into something, they are more likely to resist.*

A couple thousand years after Jesus came to model it Himself, Dutch missiologist Henrik Kraemer coined the phrase *point of contact*. This is a term defining the single-most determining factor of whether a person will be open-minded or close-minded in a conversation about God. In terms of a point of contact with secular culture, there are no magic ingredients, but if there is a single overriding component (as the respondent above accurately perceived), it is *love*. Jesus modeled it every day, and those who truly love others are far better Greatest-Story-tellers than those of us who may just be trying to put an evangelistic notch on our belt.

When asked what the greatest commandment was, Jesus answered, "Love the Lord your God with all your heart and with all your soul and with all your mind and with all your strength. The second is this: Love your neighbor as yourself. There is no commandment greater than these" (Mark 12: 30-31). Love is not only the greatest commandment, but Paul tells us in 1 Corinthians 13 that love is also the greatest gift of all.

For just one example of love in action, consider what one respondent wrote about a friend named Shannon:

> *Shannon, a twenty-something, is naturally shy and introverted, but she decided that after two years of hiding out in her apartment complex she needed to at least attempt to connect with her neighbors. She handed out flyers for some local event by knocking on doors. One of her neighbors was a young couple from India, both in doctoral programs at the local university. They were expecting their first child in that small apartment and had NOTHING. No friends, no family, no money, and no idea where to get stuff for their newborn. They were all alone and strangers in a strange land. And they were Shannon's neighbors.*
>
> *Shannon spent some time with them and then offered to throw them a baby shower. (She had to explain this strange American custom.) She got a few friends from her church and some of the other neighbors to join in on the party and provide diapers, clothing, a crib, a stroller… virtually everything that was needed. More than twenty people crowded into that tiny one-bedroom apartment and shared food and drink and laughter together.*
>
> *The apartment complex is still buzzing. So is the church that Shannon is part of. She did what was doable. Paid attention. Listened. Prayed. And then figured out a way to love her neighbors, who happened to be strangers in a foreign land. And she inspired a lot of us to look for ways to do the same.*

With Christ-like love as the key motivator and component in our contact with the secular world, Kraemer (1963) says that the actual "point of contact" is *the messenger*. This position carries with it the responsibility of having a genuine interest in the person or persons to whom the message is directed—their backgrounds, their work, their families and their worldviews. In order to find commonality with others, we must sit on the same bench with them. We must listen and probe empathetically and build relationships by being other-focused. This is love, overflowing naturally from the heart of the Spirit-led Christian.

Shannon's story shows us that one need not be captain of the cheerleading team to be empathetic, ask concerned questions, and show enthusiasm in helping and encouraging others. Shannon was an introvert and an unusually shy person, but she extended herself beyond the comfort zone of her safe-and-solo apartment. Following the prompting of the Holy Spirit and the example of Jesus, she was able to contextualize the message of Christ's love to the needs of her neighbors.

We must be mindful of contextualizing the message. There is a difference between *adapting* the message and *altering* the message. Kraemer (1957) emphasizes that restoring communication with secular culture will not happen by using more intelligible language, or devising more and more programs. Instead, he contends, the Church must recover consciousness of its true nature and calling. We, the Church, must recommit to reflecting the truth of God instead of allowing our mission and methodology to be dictated by the ways of the world.

Kraemer's indictment of American evangelism is shared by others such as Mark Noll (1995), who has asserted that the evangelical movement may have pandered so much to American culture, tried so hard to be popular, and perpetuated such a "feel-good" faith, that it has lost not only its mind but its soul.

Some, like Dan, are losing confidence in the church:

> *There is a rising tide of confused discontent in our local churches. People have a deep sense that there ought to be more to the Christian life than attending church services and activities. I feel the same way. I did as a young person growing up in church. I did in college.*

> *I thought I could make a difference as a pastor—but instead just got more overchurched. Now I'm trying to raise three children as Christians without making them overchurched—very hard when I'm still struggling. I am a firm believer in the church—I just don't like it very much.*

> *A person may be drawn to church, but he or she resists all the way. He may attend services and activities, but does not commit. He has a sense that something is very wrong with the way church is, but can't make the needed changes or doesn't know where to begin. She is told she needs to be more committed. But she wonders why she needs to be more committed to sitting and listening...why she isn't being challenged to be more committed to the way of Jesus.*

Jacques Ellul (1986) points to the many contradictions between the Bible and the practice of the Church, and asserts that what is called Christianity today is actually far removed from the intention and revelation of God through the Scriptures.

Ellul suggests that successive generations have reinterpreted the Scriptures to conform it to their own cultures, thus moving society further from the truth of the original gospel. He references Kierkegaard, who declared that nothing displeases or revolts us more than New Testament Christianity when it is properly proclaimed. The heart of the problem, according to Ellul, is that our society has not accepted the fact that Christianity is a scandal, in that the authentic New Testament meaning of being a Christian is the very opposite of what is natural to the human heart. Consequently, Ellul asserts, many people attempt to make the Christian faith acceptable and easy and, therefore, pervert its true message.

As God's chosen point of contact with those who don't know Him, it is our responsibility to make sure the integrity of the message is upheld.

Two Roads, One Choice, No Apologies

> *The Christian ideal has not been tried and found wanting. It has been found difficult and left untried.*
>
> — G. K. Chesterton

Organized religion. Now there's a stereotype. And some would even call it an oxymoron. In fact, there seems to be such an outright revolt against organized religion that the concept has been expanded to deride any group or organization that "tells you what to think or believe." It's as if the idea of a community of worship is un-American or something.

Because organized religion has become such a negative stereotype, our culture has adopted a more popular substitute they call *spirituality*. It's become a mantra of sorts, allowing people to believe in "whatever works for you." For much of secular society, this definition of spirituality is the only intelligent, freethinking way to go, and participating in a Church or an organization of like-minded people is anything from "so thirty years ago" to mental imprisonment. After all, in an age of enlightened individualism, who is God to tell us what to believe? And who is Jesus to tell us that He is the only way to God and heaven? How intolerant of us.

If the "me generation" was thirty-something years ago, then I guess the logical progression is to encroach upon God's territory and simply declare that we, sophisticated and intelligent beings that we are, have come to a better conclusion than that offered by the Bible.

> *I feel God and I have our own relationship and I know what is right from wrong, and all the religious rules don't apply to me.*
>
> — *Study respondent*

If you think about it, the same thing happened in biblical times. Classic self-idolatry. All kinds of societies throughout history thought they had figured it out, that God's way was bogus and their golden calf or other idols were the real deal. But if we read closely, we see that a frightening number of these societies came out on the wrong end of blunt instruments. Plans like theirs generally end with some serious weeping and gnashing of teeth. We need only excavate the ruins of ancient self-absorbed societies—one on top of another—to verify that such wayward pride, such "spirituality," does not last long.

People in our society like to proclaim that they are more tolerant than previous generations. Their tolerance seems to stop at biblical Christianity, so they may not be as consciously tolerant as they think. Instead they are caught in a rut of indifference, apathy, and relativism, doing their own thing to make sense of the world.

> *It's hard to believe anyone believes [in God and His Son Jesus] anymore. I'm sure people do—my friends do—but media draws a different picture.*
>
> — *Study respondent*

We who are anchored in Christ and to the wonderful, absolute truth of His Word must interrupt this meaningless direction before the powerful tide of self-worshipping relativism and spirituality sweeps away a generation.

Folks are basically opting for the path of least resistance. This is certainly a message that has become clear in my own life: "Enter through the narrow gate. For wide is the gate and broad is the road that leads to destruction, and many will enter through it. But small is the gate and narrow the road that leads to life, and only a few find it" (Matthew 7:13–14).

Two roads, Jesus taught. Only two. One's challenging; one's easy. One leads to life, the other to death. This is the antithesis of universalism, which teaches that countless roads lead to enlightenment or some higher power. But God, through His Son, couldn't have made it clearer for us: There are only two paths, and only one that gets you where you want to go.

The choice is ours. Whether consciously or not, most choose the easy way—the wide, paved, most-traveled road that leads to destruction. Selected lyrics from Randy Stonehill's song "Angry Young Men" illustrate the choice:

They say if you don't laugh you cry
I say if you don't live you die
Well, well, the road to hell is paved with some impressive alibis
But unless you thirst for Jesus first, man, heaven will pass you by
Heaven will pass you by.

You'll be tempted, tried and tested
There'll be wars the devil wins
But God's love is not a license to lie there in your sins
He understands the human heart
His mercy is complete
But His grace was not intended
As a place to wipe your feet.
He wants some angry young men
Who love the Lord they serve
Ones who'll do much more than make a speech
Ones who'll act their faith out with the passion it deserves
'Cause if we cannot live it, tell me, who are we to preach?

As my spiritual mentor once told me, the authentic Christian life is no bowl of cherries. Far from what Sigmund Freud once called a crutch for the weak, the daily Christian walk is the challenge of your life. The road less traveled is narrow and rocky, chock-full of challenges and obstacles inherent to the call of Jesus. It's our privilege to invite others to join us on the journey. Our job is to walk the talk, to live the life authentically and with integrity. We are to be love-filled points of contact among the world around us and point them to Jesus, the Savior who loves them so much that He died to welcome them into the Kingdom of God.

But we live in a time when too many of us run from this duty and calling. We're so scared of offending others—or being accused of intolerance—that we've almost diminished the gospel to, in the words of Richard Niebuhr, "a God without wrath bringing men without sin into a kingdom without judgment through the ministrations of a Christ without a cross."

As these study respondents reflect, our tolerant, open-minded, and spirituality-focused society still likes to stereotype the gospel message via outdated impressions of hellfire-and-damnation sermons and preachers:

> *They are good and bad as all other groups, but once they start getting loud and spitting out lines from the Bible, they look and sound idiotic and I shut them out.*

> *Those presentations seem store-bought and fed to those who will swallow it. They always allude to how terrible people are and how we will go to hell if we aren't "saved" and profess our devotion to the Lord.*

But really, how long has it been since you've heard one of these barnburner preachers? Not that I would rush to hear one, but it has been ages since I've heard a sermon on sin or the doctrine of hell. In fact, a recent study reported that 95 to 98 percent of those who refer to sermons of hellfire and damnation have never actually heard a sermon of this nature. These impressions are largely from hearsay, media portrayals, or what has been passed along or passed down. In other words, from stereotypes.

Walking in the Light, Walking in the World

In place of browbeating or attempting to exert superiority over those who don't know Christ, we must strike a balance, spanning boundaries that are not always clearly marked for us. We do well to accept that, as Kraemer emphasizes, the very nature of the gospel message creates a tension with which the Church has to live. He adds that the more the Church is concerned with the breakdown of communication with secular culture, the healthier it becomes. But if we adapt the message to the extent that the character of the gospel is threatened, then our efforts are rendered meaningless. This is why we must make a crystal-clear distinction between *compromising* the message and rightly *contextualizing* the message.

Sometimes half the battle is our mindset.

> *I was in line at a grocery store checkout and the lady in front of me was buying two huge bottles of vodka. I was busy having judgmental thoughts, but the cashier was busy doing what's doable. She asked the lady how she was and the lady launched into a story about her mother's illness and how she has had to care for her and the test results weren't good.*
>
> *The cashier really listened. She said things like "Oh, honey, that is so hard! Remember that God will give you the strength you need!" I was astounded by her love and care for this woman. I was lost in judgment and she was primed for love.*

An obvious challenge exists, when we attempt to be more casual or less judgmental when presenting a Christian message without compromising it. This is precisely why we must stay at the feet of Jesus, in His presence, being filled continuously with His Holy Spirit. As Kraemer proclaims in his writing, no mortal man can work faith in God in another man; the sole agent of real faith in Christ is the Holy Spirit.

To arrive at a point of contact, one must embody the likeness of Christ by having a genuine interest in the person or audience to whom the message is directed. There is really no script, formula, or setting that will always be conducive to the success of a given message at different times and places. But you and I have no authority to dilute or adapt the gospel in order to attempt to make it more pleasant. God is never made acceptable. Instead, sinners are made acceptable to God through the sacrifice of His Son.

An important finding of our study was that people are generally less defensive where spontaneity, empathy, equality, and a sense of open-mindedness about the message are present. The message is most successfully related when it flows naturally from the heart of an authentic follower of Christ, who is committed to empathizing enough to contextualize an unchanging gospel message for an ever-changing culture. An effective storyteller is one who does not rely on gimmicks, rehearsed lines, or memorized points. One must be flexible, as Kraemer says, to different persons and beliefs, as well as adaptable to a myriad of changing conditions and circumstances. More than any other factor, the point of contact is the messenger and the spirit with which he or she engages in conversation.

STEPS TO FINDING POINTS OF CONTACT BY CREATING A SUPPORTIVE COMMUNICATION CLIMATE:

COMMONALITY

Touch points and parallels: common communicative ground.

TRUST AND CREDIBILITY

Establishing a relationship though genuine dialogue and open exchange.

EMPATHY

Opportunity to listen arises by showing genuine interest.

CONTEXTUALIZING

Communicating a relevant message in the vernacular of the person or group.

— These steps are dependent upon —
Thinking → Praying → Strategizing → Acting

If the "Points of Contact" chart seems complicated, it's actually not. The following story illustrates its simple-but-powerful concept.

> *Having been in my community for only nine months, I felt the Lord wanted me to do a Thanksgiving dinner for whoever wanted to come. Since the VFW Hall sometimes lets people use their building to do a Bible study with high schoolers, I asked if I could do the dinner there and they said yes.*

What a blessed day we had, as we served over 110 people and let them see the love of God. The best part of the whole day was my roommate's friend who came to help, and was so giving in regards to doing dishes, pouring coffee, and taking dinners to the folks.

I knew he didn't know the Lord, and as we were the last two people in the building after cleaning up, I shared the gospel with him.

He was thrilled with the good news that he can be forgiven and have a relationship with our Savior, Jesus. And, that was the reason we did this dinner in the first place. As he contemplated the words I had just shared, he decided to ask Jesus into his heart. What a true Thanksgiving it was for me to see a new brother going to heaven. I'm rejoicing because [God] has me here in a small town in Oregon to do His will!"

We have the example, the methodology, and most importantly the Spirit of Christ within us to effectively share our story of faith with others. This communication need not be hurried, rushed, ill timed, or poorly placed; instead, we can confidently convey our stories from a place of communion with Christ. We find this place at the feet of Jesus, soaking up His Word, learning His ways of love, empathy, and transcendence. As we are firmly rooted in and with Christ, we are compelled to show, tell, and help others.

We so often refer to sharing Christ with others as "reaching out." This is true, but our aim is to actually make contact, to touch people. We know that we have life-giving power through the Holy Spirit who resides within us. We can reach out in faith that we *expect* to be used to touch others. As Jesus connected with tax collectors over the dinner table, we, too, can spend more time with people who are not like us. Once we understand that it is not about us but about Jesus, we can be free to truly act as a conduit as the Lord wills and directs.

It is essential that we talk to God about people before we talk to people about God. Simply ask Him, *Lord, what is Your message for this person through me at this time?* Such constant communication will assure us opportunities to interact with the right person, at the right time, in the right place. Living in Christ leads to a natural outflow to others. Having listened to the Spirit within, and listened to the other person with empathic love, we will be used by God to touch them with the love, words, encouragement, and message He has for them. This in turn increases our faith for future encounters, as we are sustained and encouraged by Luke 12:12: "For the Holy Spirit will teach you at that time what you should say."

It starts with one person, one heart.

Pray, listen, and act. And your faith will grow mightily.

FOURTEEN

Melting the Mask

Religion is for people who don't want to go to hell.
Christianity is for people who have been there.

— *Steve Brown*

"God is dead."

Almost everyone is familiar with that notorious declaration from German philosopher Friedrich Nietzsche. What we may not know about Nietzsche is that he was born the son of a Lutheran pastor in Röcken, Saxony. When asked why he had such disdain for the religion of Christianity, Nietzsche replied: "Because I never saw the people in my father's Church enjoying themselves."

To be called a hypocrite is one of the greatest insults that can be hurled against a person. Therefore, in order to avoid this label, instead of confessing our sins, we tend to hide them by pretending that no one can see our flaws. No matter the sin, great or small from our own perspective, we carry around a blanket of anxiety that we'll eventually be found out. Living like this is truly living in darkness. And obviously, it's impossible to hide such sour Christianity under a bushel.

Jekyll and Hyde

Question: *What is your opinion of Christian people?*

> *There are two types. (1) People who aren't perfect but admit they aren't and still are good people. (2) People who aren't perfect but act like they are.*

> — Study respondent

Part of our Jekyll and Hyde persona is perhaps influenced by the perception of others. Oftentimes, the assumption of non-believers is that a Christian is one who claims he or she does not sin. In reality, the opposite is the case. Admitting being a sinner is a prerequisite for being a Christian. Churches are filled with sinners. So is the world. But the world is not saved by grace until they meet Christ.

The purpose for this book is neither to defend nor condemn my brothers and sisters in Christ. Rather, it is to help us overcome that which impedes us from revealing Christ to others. We have taken a look at Christians through the eyes of others in an effort to try to understand why and how they perceive Christians as they do. There are plenty of books that make a case for Christianity, and plenty that attempt to make a case against it. We neither wish to apologize for nor point fingers of blame at hypocrites.

We seek to understand both the hypocrite and the observer of the hypocritical behavior...and to find out why one is comfortable about it and another is not. For example, a person may feel a sense of righteousness in an action that another person views as hypocrisy. This contradiction is often termed *duality*. We seek to understand why a faith that claims to be built on absolute truth can be so easily dismissed with examples of actions that seem to render moot the existence of absolutes.

In his book cited earlier, Henrik Kraemer bases the construction of his contact theory in the theology that, even in our fallen condition, man is God's creature in whose heart has been placed an eternal knowledge of God. This places man in a contradictory position, since we *seek* God, and at the same time try to run from Him. The apostle Paul describes the inner war like this: "I do not understand what I do. For what I want to do I do not do, but what I hate I do" (Romans 7:15).

This duality drives both sides (the hypocrite and the observer of the hypocrisy) into defensive postures, which has created an ongoing cultural and intellectual argument. Beneath the surface—in private discussions, in the classrooms of universities, on the 24-hour news networks, and between the governing philosophies of nations—the question of Christian duality ignites passionate feeling for and against both modern and historical Christianity. Over time, the dilemma has been explored in various forms, even as the subject of Bob Dylan's hit song, "Gotta Serve Somebody," in which he sings that everyone must choose between the devil and the Lord.

In Kraemer's view, this central dilemma of man testifies to our indestructible relatedness to God, and thus sets up an undeniable point of contact for the message of the gospel. Jesus understood His mission, and that every element of His mission was linked to His identity with God the Father. He understood that He Himself, the messenger, was the point of contact on earth. How much more are we, identified in and through Christ and enabled by His Holy Spirit, the point of contact for people today? Might we be a point of contact for people like Jodi?

> *I always wanted a father. When I was two years old, my father went*
> *away and my mother went to jail. My sister and I lived with our*
> *grandparents. We had been abused in every imaginable way, and to*

get back at my parents I started drinking and smoking. I was only eleven. I thought that no one loved me. One day a friend invited me to go to church. I didn't want to go. I knew they were going to tell me that I was soooo bad! Instead, a guest speaker drew a picture of a lighthouse. The message he gave me was that without God, I was in the dark. He will show me the way to go and He will forgive me, because HE loves me! I accepted Jesus that day. When I did, I found a FATHER who will never leave me.

This Jekyll-and-Hyde duality is the very struggle we have to continually face as we prepare ourselves to represent the message. But that's just it: we are ready once we are identified with Christ. If we contemplate the struggle too long, we'll never deem ourselves fit enough to get out there and serve.

Save Your Face

Most all of us have an ugly side. To save face has become the modus operandi of today's Christian. An embedded tradition in other cultures, saving face becomes a gray and dangerous pattern for a believer in Christ. It's a breeding ground for deceit because it serves to rationalize the practice of keeping things hidden in the dark. And we often do it under the guise of saving face on behalf of others. We can almost *taste* the hypocrisy; it hits home because we have all done it. For instance, perhaps the pastor who failed to show for dinner at Donnie's felt that he was saving face by publicly apologizing to Donnie and his family in a church service later the same night.

Attempting to save face from our flaws is perhaps the greatest inhibitor of finding the freedom in Christ promised in the Scriptures. In fact, I'm only recently beginning to understand for myself what this freedom means. For example, in John 8, Christ confronted the prostitute and actually stated what her sin was. Yet in so doing, Jesus set her free and made her feel completely and totally loved. He spoke in absolute truth and in absolute confidence. There were no veiled references, no condemnation. Only love.

If someone like Carla visits your church next Sunday, would she feel welcome? How would you reach out to her during or after the service?

I was twenty-one, unmarried, pregnant, and into drugs and alcohol. One day a friend asked me to go to church with her. I told her that the only dress I had was a disco dress that was really short. She said that was okay because "God doesn't look on the outside."

The preaching was unlike anything I had ever heard before. I listened, and by the end, my heart was pounding and the preacher was giving the call for sinners to come to the Lord. With no cares of how I was dressed, I went to the altar and fell to my knees and began crying. Then I asked Jesus Christ to come into my life and cleanse me of my sins and make me whole. I felt a warmth and knew that Jesus had made me into a new creation.

Despite what we read or hear, beyond the labels and stereotypes, people are still watching us. It is clear that people want to see authentic Christians and how we work through everyday trials and temptations by faith. If it doesn't seem to work for us, why would they want to sign up? Let's face it: Why would we want what most Christians portray or project?

Again, we cannot look at this only collectively; we must personalize it. We must examine ourselves and how we live, think, speak, and act. Is the faith you portray something that will truly attract others to check into?

It's also time for us to be open about struggle and failure. It is what we hide in the dark that makes one hypocritical when it's exposed involuntarily. All humans struggle, but as Christians, we can witness even through our failures and weaknesses. Christianity offers perfection in the form of Christ, for people who are imperfect.

Paul brings us to this epiphany in 2 Corinthians 12:8, quoting Jesus Himself: "My grace is sufficient for you, for my power is made perfect in weakness." This is a life-altering passage for the believer identified in Christ—a paradox the world will never comprehend: "For when I am weak, then I am strong" (v. 10).

It's a paradox that, through the eyes of our masks, is just as foreign to many Christians.

Melting the Mask

When we have the courage to become broken, on our knees at the feet of Jesus, pride dissipates like vapor in His presence. Suddenly the Holy Spirit removes our will, our self—the "me" of it all—from the equation and we can see the power of honest vulnerability and humility taking over.

It's impossible for us to remove the mask, you see. Rather, it is gradually melted off...in the presence of I AM, in and through identification with Him.

To face our own sin, the ugly side of our intensely personal hypocrisy, is the beginning of the melting of the mask. At the feet of Jesus we surrender the constant human effort and all of our striving to save face. We surrender our pride, which is the mask itself.

Do not fool yourself by picturing a sleek mask worn once a year for a Mardi Gras party. Mine, and yours, is more like the iron box Leonardo DiCaprio's character Philippe languishes under in the film *Man in the Iron Mask*. In order to prevent an overthrow of his throne, King Louis

XIV, in an act of utter betrayal and hypocrisy, concealed the identity of his twin brother Philippe by having a large iron mask locked over his head. The innocent man was imprisoned in solitary confinement for life. That's the kind of mask I'm talking about.

We all have borne this mask at different times in life. Though a cumbersome disguise, it is one with which we become increasingly comfortable, and thus breaking free can be very painful. The shame that comes from exposure can be debilitating. But admission, understanding, accountability, and forgiveness are pivotal steps toward freedom from the mask.

> *I was a very lonely and unhappy person inside, full of pain, anger, resentment. Then I heard the gospel of Jesus Christ. I accepted Him as my Lord and Savior and instantly had peace in my heart and have been a new person since.*
>
> — *Study respondent*

As Philippe was finally rescued by the musketeers, so too can we be liberated. Imagine the true communion we will enjoy with the Lord with the burdensome mask cast aside: "But if we walk in the light, as he is in the light, we have fellowship with one another, and the blood of Jesus, His Son, purifies us from all sin" (1 John 1:7). Imagine the freedom with which you will now view yourself *in* Christ. The victory over duality is won. Imagine how you are unencumbered to freely share with others, without getting yourself in the way—sharing your true self in freedom and abandonment, showing your true face.

Our Calling: Transparency

No wonder people have difficulty understanding and feeling what we believe, or seeing who we are. With our masks *on*, we are not ourselves at all—but are merely in character playing a role. In and of ourselves, we are outside the fullness of Christ in us. But with our masks *off*, we are *in* Christ, identified with Him in His presence, in His suffering, in His death, in His resurrection, in His life…and in His empathy and yearning for others to know Him as we do. It is only through authentic, mask-off identification in Christ that we are worthy to represent Him and His sacred message to other people. It is only with masks *off* that we are given eyes to see that living the Christian life is pointless with masks *on*.

Through identification with Christ, we are able to confront our own sin with complete honesty. We can only become free of sin when we come face to face with Jesus, knowing and recognizing that we are sinners in need of daily redemption.

> *We come face to face with Jesus when we can look at the cross and say, "I did that to Him and He did that for me."*
>
> — *D. T. Niles*

To present, or represent, anything else to others is heresy. This is why unbelievers do not know the true message: We fail to represent the gospel as flawed individuals saved by grace, walking in freedom because of Jesus Christ. This is also why many Christians don't get the message either. We use our own devices and efforts, trying so hard to portray a walk of freedom, and the result is that we end up exhausted. Consequently, we show every bit of *ourselves* to others, instead of pointing them to the author of our faith. Observers toss all Christians into a category. Call it what you will—stereotyping, pigeonholing, labeling—but we are all viewed as one large group. They know this group has a standard, but they do not see us collectively living up to this standard.

Problem is, they have no idea of the rationale or spirit behind why we aim for the top. And assuredly, they never will as long as we leave it with the group. It must be a personal, individual problem. Yours and mine. One heart, one life at a time, we must drop the mask and become transparent believers. Are you courageous enough to even *glimpse* into the mirror of transparency? If the people who are watching us feel that we are humans trying to live up to a standard of men, then we are destined to fail. But if they see that we are sinful individuals in daily need of surrender and redemption to a personal God far greater than ourselves, then we open the door to the work of the Holy Spirit.

You may be thinking, *Well, I'm not the one judging and condemning others, so it's not my problem.* But that way of thinking is precisely the problem. Just as we need to represent true freedom to unbelievers, we must also have empathy and passion for fellow believers who are mispresenting or misrepresenting the message. We must be salt, light, and freedom to our fellow Christians so that they can in turn influence others to be truthful representatives of our Lord. Acts 20:28 instructs that we must be shepherds to the church of God which He purchased with His own blood. In order to represent and spread His message of redemption, God puts His name on the church—on *people*, not on institutions or buildings. This is where our individual communion with Christ affects the greater communication of the collective group.

Identification with other people—Christian and non-Christian— flows naturally from identity in the Lord. In turn, the essence of identification with others is simply *love*. Christ became sin for us. In a similar way, when we sincerely identify with others, we meet them where they are and contextualize the message by following the example of Jesus. This is the true meaning of empathy.

Here is a very practical commitment for you and me in the days, months, and years ahead:

- I will put people concerns higher than institutional concerns.

- I will be accountable to God and my close associates for doing so.

- I will monitor my daily and weekly activities to make sure I am moving toward people who need Jesus.

With our masks off, other Christians will pray for us because we are open with them. Nonbelievers will see themselves and their own struggles within us, which creates a bridge for communication and approachability. The most effective thing we can do is to offer a genuine community that identifies with others and helps them experience the transforming love of God through Jesus Christ. Collectively, the church—every local church within the universal church—needs to become a hospital for the spiritually sick. Christianity represents a higher calling and a higher path—providing the discipline, community, accountability, and forgiveness to walk in transparent liberation.

Your Calling: Transparent Action

Living in this spirit of freedom gives us greater willingness to transparently confront problems, conflict, and grudges. With courage to approach people in these situations, we often find that people are quick to forgive. Why? Because deep down, we know that to forgive is the right thing to do. How new and good and clean it feels to be in right relationship with others, to bury the hatchet and breathe again. Is there someone you need to approach in transparent fashion to seek or grant forgiveness? Ask the Lord to help you visit or call someone today. I promise, if you do so with a humble spirit, you will experience untold freedom.

And if you think person-to-person restoration is good, consider how much more our heavenly Father is ready and willing to forgive a contrite heart. Think how quickly we can restore our relationship with Him through His unconditional forgiveness. Contemplate how marvelous it is that we are allowed to restore relationship with God— not on conditional terms, but with a completely new, clean, and fresh start that gives us the privilege of re-entering into true communion with our precious Lord.

Because of this intimate relationship with God, we all have a Christian love story. Regardless of our past experiences, we all have a story to share and that others want to hear:

My testimony is not amazing. I have not been healed of cancer or cured from heroin [addiction]. To some, it may even be boring. But God has shown me that my testimony is sweet. I was born into a Christian family that has always shown me God's love.

God has protected me from so many things. Still, I have stumbled. But God, through His grace, has always brought me back in His arms. He is truly an awesome God!

This walk seems so long sometimes, and it gets so hard. But God said that it's going to be okay, it's going to be all right! Just hang in there, whatever your life may be, whatever your testimony may be. God is there with you, and what has happened in your life, God uses it for good. So be thankful for your testimony. It is unique and no one has one just like it, so it will be something that may bless others and you in the future!

When we are in the right place in our relationship with God, we have a peace about our daily life and our choices. This is what it means to follow Christ in terms of what God created you to do. It is important to follow your passions, gifts, and that gut feeling, instead of choosing your life based only on what's safe or practical. Callings come in all shapes and sizes, and with blatant disregard for our own timetables. What we *can* expect is disruption in the form of a direction God intends, and one that might be outside of our conception. So the question for action is, *What is your calling for today, at this very moment? And how will you share it to help and encourage others?*

Can People See It in You?

> *Preach the Gospel at all times, and when necessary use words.*
> – *St. Francis of Assisi*

We are the representation of God's glory on earth.

What a responsibility ... and what an honor! But take a moment and think about what it evokes within you. Joy or pressure? Adequacy or inadequacy? Or perhaps *Great, I can't wait*, or *Whoa, I'm not ready*.

But if we really are the representation of God's glory on earth, can people see it? And if they can't, how will they? If we don't show them Jesus, how are they going to see Him? We are the only living representatives on the face of the earth to shine the light of God's glory through His Son.

In our biblically-illiterate society, non-Christians do not read the Bible—they read us. And if they read you and me verbatim, may they see a sign that points them away from our flawed humanity and toward the perfect model, Jesus.

If we don't show them, they won't see. If we don't tell them, they won't hear.

This is really the only reason that a cure for the epidemic of hypocrisy is critical. If the church is in decay and in need of revival, then we, the people of God, are in decay and in need of revival. Reformation of the church begins with personal, individual revival. The breakdown is in the heart of each individual; therefore, restoration lies within the heart of each person as well.

Together in this book, we have journeyed back to square one in an effort to know more of God's character, and to worship God not for what He can do for us, but because of who He is. Jesus said, "What the Father does, I will do also" (Matthew 4:19). Through His Son Jesus, our identity must be in the Father, to embrace His love and sacrifice. And through this transformation, God's love becomes part and parcel of our very being—such that we can't help but be affected.

This authentic communion with our heavenly Father makes us who we are in Christ to the extent that everything we think, do, and say is representative of Him. Jesus is not here in bodily form, so people look to us to represent Him. We must help them. We must show them Jesus. This is how we "show them the Father." It is our mission, our calling, our great privilege.

> *Arise, shine, for your light has come, and the glory of the LORD rises upon you.*
>
> *See, darkness covers the earth and thick darkness is over the peoples, but the LORD rises upon you and His glory appears over you. Nations will come to your light, and kings to the brightness of your dawn.*
>
> *— Isaiah 60:1–3*

We are the representation of God's glory on earth. Arise and shine! We have the joy and privilege of representing the greatest message ever delivered—a message of hope, redemption, and freedom.

Through the death of Christ, our sin is atoned for, and we can be free from hypocrisy through identification in Jesus.

And just as Christ met us where we are, we can find common ground with others. Through empathy and transparency, we can listen and share burdens, directing others to the only answer: Jesus Christ. Sitting at His feet, we simply invite others to join us there. To look up, seek His face, soak up His words, and follow Him.

But God doesn't want you to *stay* at His feet. The more we seek and worship the Lord for who He is, our faith in Him will grow until we *stand* in His presence. He desires for us to see Him face-to-face.

We begin by acknowledging and knowing Him as King. That in itself is glorious, but He wants to take us further. He wants us to know Him not only as King, but as heavenly Bridegroom. He desires for us to *fall in love* with Him, to know Him as the Beloved, the lover of our souls and He whom our souls love. True communion with Him is the purest and fullest expression of this love affair. Communion is giving God the "stuff" of our lives. Everything. God says, "Take me, eat and drink of me." There is no greater intimacy known to man.

Back to the Beginning

Trust God first. Place Him at the very center of your life. When you do, the focus is removed from yourself.

Hasten back to the beginning. Back to God, and back to your first glimpse of Jesus—returning to the joy and fervor of your salvation. This is what I have deliberately done in these pages. I have reached back not only to feel but to be embraced by the tapestry of this powerful and tender atmosphere—the days, weeks, and months surrounding the day of my salvation as well as the other seasons of special growth in my Christian walk.

This prolonged revisitation, which is available to us at any time, has flooded my being with thoughts, memories, praises, emotions and petitions—all the core attributes of the relationships most meaningful to us. How truly privileged we are to enter into such an intimate relationship with the maker of heaven and earth, our precious Lord.

And it is all so real, like a wonderful aroma revisited. Unmistakable. You can evoke these sacred experiences just as I have, through the signs and symbols inevitably marking your own unique journey: the power of song and lyric, recollections of moving stories from the past, or poignant words spoken by special people whom the Lord has placed in your path.

From time to time, reaching back to visit our foundation is essential. When we take time to reflect and meditate in this way, we are reminded of the grace by which we firmly stand in our identity through Christ Jesus so that our next steps are affirmed by what God has laid before us.

And this will take us back to the feet of Jesus, where the journey daily begins. There we can surrender ourselves and trust His message to impact others. Trust God with all your life, even unto death. Give Him everything without cutting corners. Check yourself in the mirror while keeping your eyes on Him. Then you will be able to trust that His message will flow naturally from your fullness into the lives of others.

We can successfully end personal hypocrisy if our eyes are fixed on the author of the message and the perfecter of our faith. Only then are we able to point people away from ourselves and to the perfect representative of our faith, Christ alone.

The challenge of removing the mask is profound. The problem did not arise overnight, and thus the remedy is a journey of ongoing devotion. It is neither an arrival nor a destination, but a journey of commitment instead of contentment.

This is why *"All the Damn Christians"* was such an introspective struggle of self-examination for me to complete. I have found that I'm only beginning to discover the right path. But with each step, I know that in my journey I am anything but alone.

I pass this challenge along to you to begin your own journey, and that you might in turn, challenge others to begin theirs.

One heart, one life at a time.

Appendix A
The Survey

Thank you for your important contribution to this research. Please be honest in your explanations. It will take 10–15 minutes to complete the questionnaire. If you find that a particular question does not apply to you or that you may not wish to answer, please skip to the next question. All information and results are confidential. This research purposes to interpretatively measure the attitudes, opinions, and stereotypes of people toward the religion of Christianity, its followers, and the message that they supposedly represent.

1.   What is your age?

2.   What is your gender?

3.   Do you consider yourself a spiritual person?

4.   Do you consider yourself a religious person?

5.   If you subscribe to a particular religion or spirituality, what is it?

6.   Briefly explain why you have made this choice and indicate how long you have believed this way.

7.   What role does your belief thus play in your life in terms of routines and practices such as prayer, meditation, and worship, etc.?

8.   If you do not subscribe to any religion or spirituality, briefly explain your reasoning for this choice and indicate how long you have believed this way.

9. Have you ever changed your views on your own spirituality (for example, changed religion or belief system), and if so, what brought about that change?

10. How do you feel about the phrase, "America is a Christian nation"?

11. What is your opinion of the religion of Christianity?

12. What is your opinion of Christian people?

13. Please explain how you feel that your opinions may have been influenced by media images or stereotypes.

14. The message of Christianity is often referred to as the "gospel of Jesus Christ." Can you recall hearing or reading a presentation of the "gospel"?

15. Through which medium (spoken message, TV, radio, literature, etc.) have you experienced this type of presentation?

16. Briefly describe how the message was presented.

17. Honestly, how did you react to this presentation?

18. If you chose to accept the presentation, which factors were most significant in forming the basis of your decision?

19. If you chose to reject the presentation, which factors were most significant in forming the basis of your decision?

20. In your opinion, how could the presentation have been improved?

21. Did this presentation change your opinion of Christianity in any way?

22. If you were to hear the content of this presentation again, where (in which setting), and how (through which medium) would you be most open to hearing it?

Please be sure to answer this question:

23. Briefly state the "gospel" (Christian message) the way you understand it to be.

"All the Damn Christians"

Appendix B
Survey Results

For our study of contemporary attitudes toward Christianity, we surveyed college-age students from a variety of backgrounds on two university campuses: one in the Southeast and one on the West Coast. We received 682 completed questionnaires. The following is a representative sampling of the questions and their responses.

Survey Question 8

If you do not subscribe to any religion or spirituality, briefly explain your reasoning for this choice and indicate how long you have believed this way.

1. I have not chosen a religion because when I was younger (elementary) I was forced to go to the same place and believe in what my grandma did, which was Jehovah's Witness [sic]. Now that I'm older, I have to find myself.

2. I just don't know. I'd like to believe there is something divine, but you have to prove it. Four years ago.

3. I don't think organized religion makes sense. I don't understand if there is one God, why are there so many different beliefs and stories about Him? I have believed this way for roughly three years.

4. I don't accept the Bible as truth. I don't think a benevolent God would allow so much evil.

5. Personally, I view religion as a great way to learn morals and respect. However, I feel people get hope from religion, a hope that I do not need. I am strong on my own.

6. I don't fit in with any one religion. I have a wide range of beliefs.

7. I find it difficult to limit my way of life per some doctrine. I also feel that organized religion is too controlling and authoritative.

8. I believe that religion ultimately divides people. Its perpetuation is based on teaching its beliefs to kids at a young age. Generally, people believe what their parents believe, so it's sad we are divided by something that we might not even have believed in if born into a different family.

9. There are no facts in life that make religion true. I feel that it is all imaginary, such as heaven, afterlife, rebirth, etc.

10. I believe religion is a crutch for people who are afraid of dying. Like all religion, it is a myth, perpetuated by fear of death. "Faith" is a poor excuse to negate science, and it just shows ignorance.

11. I'm agnostic because I believe that the purpose of the belief in some higher being is to find a spirituality and a way of life for yourself; that is to say that all religions should fulfill the same purpose rather than create segregation amongst believers.

12. At this point in my life, I'm far too concerned with "earthly" enjoyments to become preoccupied with the beyond over the immediate.

13. I truly believe that church/religion and the Bible was written [sic] by men and does not speak about women in a right way.

Survey Question 10

How do you feel about the phrase "America is a Christian nation"?

1. I feel like everyone believes in God.

2. I'm not too sure because I'm from Ireland. What I have noticed about the Bible belief of Mississippi is people say they are Christians but really they aren't. They just go to church.

3. I guess that I can say America was supposedly based on Christianity, but mankind sometimes uses the Bible to justify ungodly acts like slavery. So, is America a Christian nation? Yes and no.

4. I feel that America is becoming like Sodom and Gomorrah because people are so blinded by false prophets. They are gullible and Satan is seeking to destroy our nation piece by piece. He has already taken prayer out of schools, and legalized same-sex marriages (this is an abomination to God our Creator). God spews this out of His mouth!

5. I don't feel as if America is a Christian nation sometimes because there is a lot of hatred and killing in America, and Christians don't do that.

6. I think that for the most part that gives a bad name to Christianity and to Christ. There are so many un-Christian things about our country and so many people who are against it now that I don't know how it is considered that. It's not Christian in the truest since of the word at least.

7. It's a joke. It should read, America was a Christian nation. We can't claim this while allowing gays to marry, abortion, etc., and also not allow God into schools and courts.

8. That is how it is. Americans are more interested in the "Christian" way instead of the peaceful one.

9. America was founded as a Christian nation, but more and more citizens of America are of different religions and America has moved toward a melting pot of religions.

10. Well, I think that it is not entirely true—our main moral "code" may be based on Christianity, but there are many other religions and cultures in our world today.

11. It's absolute total crap. America is several different things, not just one thing.

12. A true statement, but we are quickly having that taken away. Although I do not subscribe to a Christian religion, I do believe in the Christian values system.

13. Certainly, most people here at least claim to be Christian. And I do feel that Christianity influences our government too much, and at the same time, not enough. For example, our government leaders DO NOT exhibit the ideas of grace and forgiveness, which should be important to real Christians.

14. I detest the phrase since America has left its Christian roots both spiritually and politically; many Americans identify themselves as Christians who are not.

15. I feel that it's overused and trite and is not a true representation. I feel it's hypocritical because many people say they're Christian but in fact are not (They don't live like it.)

16. I feel offended, oppressed and disgusted. I have no problem with Christianity, but America = freedom. There is a separation between church and state and therefore I should not be subjected to the tyranny of any religion that does not and should not govern my life.

17. Partly, I feel angered at its exclusivity and true tradition of sometimes very racist/supremacist attitudes that come from this statement. Partly, I feel it is true because so many of the people in the U.S. subscribe to the Christian religion.

18. The United States likes to present itself as a moral nation in order to push their agenda. It's being Christian is only a front for its real motives.

19. It's hard to believe anyone believes anymore. I'm sure people do—my friends do—but media draws a different picture.

20. I think it ignores everyone who is not Christian, but then again America has a history of excluding everyone who is non-white/non-Christian.

21. I don't like that statement. I feel it is a prejudiced statement. By America's very nature, being a land of immigrants, it should be a nation of all faiths. To subscribe [sic] it to one is exclusionary and violates the separation of church and state.

22. F------ bull---; white propaganda; these ideologies are the ones destroying the U.S.

23. One can assume that the founders of America are a certain branch of Christianity—Protestantism. But over all, much of the world is a kind of Christian microcosm because of western globalization and imperialism.

24. It makes me sick.

25. Conjures images of bigotry, hypocrisy, the Moral majority, etc. Christianity is about unconditional love and acceptance. I don't see this.

26. I think it is misrepresentative and supremacist to a certain extent.

27. I don't agree with it. There are many Christians in America, but I wouldn't link Christianity and America if asked to describe America.

Survey Question 11
What is your opinion of the religion of Christianity?

1. I believe it is the only true religion. In no other religion were miracles performed nor did the founder rise from the dead.

2. It is a 2,000-year-old "newer" version of the Jewish faith, with a much more relaxed atmosphere than many other religions.

3. Christianity is important to my life. It helps to give meaning and purpose to my life. I don't accept that I should practice "The Great Commission." Everyone doesn't need saving. People should choose what is right for them.

4. Christianity is great. Believing in God is something that I do not or will never regret. But just being "religious" is not going to get you anywhere. You have to know God on a personal level.

5. It is a business.

6. I believe that Christianity is the truth. It, in terms of its structures, has been tainted through time in culture but it is still the truth.

7. I am awestruck at the vast differences of Christianity among the denominations. I have only been to a Baptist service other than attending my church. I think it is very strange how many call themselves Christians, yet each practices in a different way.

8. I have been a Christian my whole life and most of my friends are. I'll continue being a Christian no matter what. I am so thankful that there is a God who loves and cares for us, and that we are not alone in this world. Having heaven to look forward to is wonderful. It all makes being a Christian worthwhile. However, I believe people should be told more of the good of Christianity. So often, much of what we hear about Christianity is negative, especially in our media. I think it's sad when non-Christians decide that it is offensive and unfair to them when we pray in public or talk to them about Jesus. It's sad, people have the power to take away the very foundation of our country.

9. Christianity is a person's own personal belief about a piece of history and literature. Christianity is a wonderful religion, but it is not above another religion. All religions are equal.

10. I generally dislike monotheistic religions—they're too bossy, unquestioning, conforming.

11. It's a nice mythology for those that need it.

12. Selfish, ignorant, control system.

13. I think there are some good things, some not-so-good things about it. Some myth, some truth, like every religion.

14. I believe that it blinds people, and it holds back society from evolving into a better one by prohibiting change.

15. I believe it is a wonderful religion, but one must have strong faith to be a complete believer. Many people refuse this religion because of discrepancies between science and the Bible, but with an open mind, one may see the two can coexist.

16. People have a lot of misconceptions brought about by bad examples, but it is the only way to heaven and it changed my life for the better.

17. Christianity as a religion stumbles a lot of people, but Christianity as a lifestyle is more important.

18. I believe that it is the truth. However, I also believe that there are preconceptions and generalizations made about Christianity that turn people off. It is not supposed to be a legalistic religion but rather a personal relationship with Jesus Christ.

19. I think it's a different way of life that I can't quite relate to. A central focus of Christianity is suffering and that seems like an eerie association for me.

20. In the past, it's played a huge role in the subordination of many different groups, but now with its incorporation of liberation theology, it's changed for the better.

21. Like any religion, it is a good basis for morals and values whose practices need to be tempered by common sense and pragmatism; I think Christianity is among the more sensible and equalitarian religions that exist today.

22. It is for sheep.

23. Decent; a lot of gaps, which can only be explained with faith yet could be disproved by science.

24. It's great for those who believe in it. But religion over all is a crutch for those who do not want to be personally responsible for their own actions.

25. I suppose they do an amount of significant charity work, but probably always with the additional motive of proselytizing, as well. I think Christianity contributes to a huge amount of intolerance and prejudice in the world.

26. Like most religions, the foundations and practices sound good on paper, but the reality brings about much hypocrisy and downright lying as well as judgmental beliefs to others.

27. I believe it to be too focused on the devil and sin as a motivation for being good and for praising God. It seems to discriminate against gay people and I do not ascribe to faith that discriminates and judges.

28. I think it tries to force its views too much on others (Christian TV, Christian youth groups, etc.). I also think it's become more "trendy"; that people (some youth) only practice because they've never questioned otherwise.

29. It is the cause of more death, despair, and unhappiness than any other belief.

30. Mind control, frightening, oppressive, anti-feminist, hateful.

31. I think it's somewhat naïve, believing in immaculate conception and Christ as God. But I think people should believe whatever they like, yet keep it to themselves.

32. I would have a much higher regard for the religion itself if it weren't for all the damn Christians!

33. The biggest business ever.

34. Total cult—weird and way too into their religion —scary and freaky.

Survey Question 12
What is your opinion of Christian people?

1. I believe the term "Christian" is widely misused today. It should represent followers of Christ, but mostly means nothing or just a "good person" today.

2. I believe that not all Christians are back-stabbing, gossiping people who try to bring our religion down on you. A lot of times, we are misrepresented and we all make mistakes. We are all human.

3. There are two types. (1) People who aren't perfect but admit they aren't and still are good people. (2) People who aren't perfect but act like they are.

4. My opinion is that most are probably very loving, caring, responsible individuals. Some will always try to impose their will on others, which is not in accordance with the Scriptures.

5. Christian people are good and kind, not the fanatics we are made out to be on television and in the news.

6. Yes, we are all hypocrites, and while we're alive, we always will be because we're sinners. A lot of people claim to be Christians more because of culture than faith. But there are some whose faith is truly evident and give a good witness for Christ.

7. Some you can tell they're Christian and some you can't. I think all Christians should know and understand that when you give your life to Christ, you should repent of your sins, resolve to change your life and live for Him, and then do it. For the most part, I've had good experiences with other Christians. What I don't understand is people who call themselves Christians and then say Catholics are not Christians, when, in fact, we are. I have not known any personally, but I know people who do know some like that. I think basically most Christians are good

people—some are just somewhat misguided.

8. You can believe whatever you want. It doesn't have any effect on me. Unless you're obsessive and try to push it on me.

9. Too many are Christian "for show" (my judgment of that is wrong to say) but that harms the religion more than anything else.

10. "Christian people," I believe, aren't really the kind of people that I want to embody because there aren't any real Christians in this world.

11. They're too busy trying to save everyone else's souls but their own.

12. Yikes!! Good and bad, I personally stay away from finding out if a person is of any religious affiliation.

13. Some are good, some are bad, some are okay, some are big, some are tall, some are hairy, some have dogs. They're just people.

14. They can be very judgmental and a lot of them would just assume [sic] kill off all non-believers like they have tried in the past. I think they want their religion running the country.

15. I think a lot of Christian people are too religious and so traditional that they miss the true meaning of what a Christian is.

16. Every religion has its strong believers who are good examples and believers that don't behave in a way fitted to their religion. Many church-going Christians are very loving and warm, but of course there are some who are hypocritical and condescending.

17. I know sometimes people have a reputation for being hypocrites and it frustrates me because we aren't perfect. That's why we need Jesus. People need to look past this. The church has sinners.

18. It differs depending upon their interpretation of the faith (i.e. fundamentalists/evangelicals bother me greatly), whereas many older denominations of the church bother me far less.

19. They are trying to live godly lives in a generally secular society, and [are] unfortunately sometimes perceived as hypocrites.

20. They are lazy about standing up for their beliefs, or they are pushy. They do not work together effectively. They tend to be more worldly than spiritual and therefore do not make a convincing testimony.

21. In general, the Christian people I know are good people, people like anyone else. I don't take it personally when they overstep their bounds— they can be zealous like no other—but I don't let them get away with it either.

22. They are made up of a broad spectrum of people—some of whom represent the faith accurately but others who try and force /preach the religion onto others unwillingly, giving other Christians a bad name and a reputation for being overbearing and cult-like.

23. Insecure, dependent on the idea of a guiding force as the only reason why things happen. They accept events without questioning or looking too much into it. Also, judgmental, often to the point where they condemn and are hypocritical.

24. Half of them just say they're Christians but don't even know the Bible or follow their beliefs. My roommate is a "Christian" and a lush.

25. They are hypocritical and don't even read their own religious texts. But that's only some. There are some nice Christians too.

26. Misled, like people of all religions; brainwashed, but probably with good intentions; so, no different from the Jews, Hindus, Buddhists, Islam, etc.

27. On the whole, Christians who actively follow the teachings of the New Testament are generous, kind, and moral. However, I disapprove of those evangelicals who emphasize faith and dogma to the exclusion of active engagement in this world.

28. Some are cool, but many who throw it in my face piss me off. They are usually the ones accosting me at school trying to get me to convert and not understanding that I don't believe. I don't push my atheist beliefs on anyone, why should they. The Christians I like are cool because they may have their beliefs but don't push it on me or anyone else.

29. The focus of Christianity and its followers seems to be more punitive by nature, whereas Buddhism is more of a philosophy of life.

30. I am really tired of Jehovah's Witnesses or Christians telling me I am going to go to hell. I'm fine with them as long as they don't impose their beliefs on me and they are open-minded. Christian clubs—some tend to resemble cults and people need to realize some aren't looking for God.

31. Misguided, ill-informed and terrified of free and open thought.

32. I have met good ones and bad ones. The good ones don't proselytize; they are tolerant if not loving and accepting. The bad ones are hypocrites. They're the ones that preach against gays and followers of different faiths, and can be seen sinning all the time.

33. Without them our society cannot exist; they are the vessels of God through which (today as throughout history) He fulfills His purpose for all mankind. We are being persecuted worldwide and especially within our own country—[in] the U.S. it is almost as if Christianity and their beliefs are trying to be exterminated by radical groups and the media.

34. Even as a Christian, I have a negative image of Christians in general as hypocrites and always preaching about hell. I think grace is not emphasized enough.

35. It depends; I have a great deal of respect of quietly spiritual and religious people; on the other hand, I am very turned off by "Bible thumpers" and superficially religious people. I also am very disgusted by hypocrisy of people who purpose to be religious (outwards), yet behave immorally.

36. They are good and bad as all other groups, but once they start getting loud and spitting out lines from the Bible, they look and sound idiotic and I shut them out.

37. If they try to push their ideas on other people, then I think they are annoying and wrong. If they say people are going to hell because they practice such and such behavior/religion, I think they are immoral. But if they practice their religion not doing those, I have a lot of respect.

Survey Question 13

Please explain how you feel that your opinions may have been influenced by media images or stereotypes.

1. Morals, in general, are taking a 700-mile-per-hour nosedive these days because of the media. Sex and violence run rampant through all outlets of media. It is an utter disgrace.

2. I get angry at the way the media looks down at Christianity. (e.g. The Passion [of the Christ]) It makes me mad that other religions are OK to talk about, but when you talk about God, it's almost as if people are scared of Him. It makes me so sad.

3. My beliefs come from my family, but I compromise my beliefs many times because it is not "the thing to do." It is just easier to do what is on television and what the majority of people are doing.

4. To say that Christians are all good, are all hypocritical, is a stereotype that is entirely false, but claimed every day as an excuse to ignore it.

5. It is difficult to say that my opinions have been influenced by the media, because my beliefs come from involvement in Christianity. I do think that the media tries to be anti-Christian. They are tolerant of all religions, races, sexual preferences, but for some reason aren't tolerant of Christianity.

6. They have not been. It has never been cool to be a Christian, but it is the best thing that has ever happened to my life.

7. Stereotypes—"Bible-banging Baptist"—God keeps "laying things on their hearts" to do stuff until they do something stupid or wrong, then it's "the devil, the devil did it!" I'm not too fond of Baptists as a breed.

8. I believe, with the help of media and stereotypes, that I've been influenced by thinking all Baptists condemn people to hell and the Islam religion is a truly evil religion.

9. Actually, my opinions of the Catholic church have become stronger since all of the allegations of molestation. It is in events such as these that you resort back to your core beliefs and realize that you can't let the 1 percent of the population ruin what the other 99 percent believe.

10. In my high school there were a lot of "Christian" people, but I know on the weekends they were the ones sleeping around and doing the most drugs.

11. I often feel annoyed with the Christian community for the hypocrisy displayed most prominently in the media. I also feel that the media is unfair in its representation; almost as if they go out of their way to find the poor examples and stereotypes of a group.

12. Media often portrays religious people as fanatics and they are not all like that. Not everybody is [a] religious nutcase.

13. Media definitely stereotypes all across the board—race, religion, age. I honestly wish they wouldn't and I don't like it any, it only enforces negative stereotypes across the nation.

14. I'm repelled by the media's portrayal of Christians as condemning, fanatical, and not capable of having fun.

15. Actually, the media prompts me to think completely opposite of what they project. The media is totally liberal and leftist and biased against Christians. Most of society is.

16. I know that the media likes to portray us as harsh, unforgiving, blunt, disapproving, and all that because of issues that have arisen in the 20th and 21st century about homosexuality, etc. But, I acknowledge that in the family of believers, different people react in ways that are not edifying or pleasing to God, and that makes us come off as closed-minded.

17. Even though I'm a Christian, I've picked up negative stereotypes, especially of religious right and super-conservative Christians as extreme and rule-bound and close-minded.

18. I've grown up studying about the persecution of my own people. I've learned a lot on why Jews have been scapegoated as Christ killers, etc. I've always grown up feeling that my nice, white Christian neighbor still believes devoutly that I "was going to hell."

19. Media images of Bible-thumping Christians are far from the day-to-day Christians I know. Focusing so much on extremists leaves viewers with a bad taste in their mouth when they say the word "Christian."

20. I think the media has given me the impression that most Christians are undereducated people from small rural towns in Middle America, or rich conservative bigoted white men, or people who aren't flexible in their opinions and want to convert you, too.

21. I think that too often conservative Christian fundamentalists occupy the media's interest and project a stereotypical notion of what it means to be Christian, as something anti-modern. This fuels the culture war, I think, more than anything in the teachings of Christ.

22. I think the media has portrayed Christianity as the most popular/desirable religion.

23. Well, recently on campus, many strong believing Christians speak about the Bible and campaign against liberal actions. They do impact me, like abortion and chastity, etc. I am persuaded to agree with their views.

Survey Question 14

The message of Christianity is often referred to as the "gospel of Jesus Christ." Can you recall hearing or reading a presentation of the "gospel"?

1. Yes, but I forgot what it was about.

2. Yes, most of my life. It did not always make since [sic] to me.

3. Yes, in church and listening to my stepmom.

4. I have heard that as a reference, probably through the media.

5. If you mean preaching there are too many to count.

6. Yes, I suppose.

7. No, I haven't.

8. During TLC specials on Jesus, the life of Jesus.

9. I've seen it presented on those Sunday morning religious shows when I was younger (I was disappointed cartoons weren't on; I was 10).

10. Yes, gospel means "good news" so any daily "good news" is the gospel of Jesus.

11. Yes, when I wrote my history theories on Quakers.

12. No, have not attended a presentation of the gospel.

13. Not really, I tend to tune out those messages.

Survey Question 16

Briefly describe how the message was presented.

1. It's all entertainment. They are forced to make it semi-appealing. Too much propaganda.

2. Praise and worship and then a speaker explaining the will of God and that He is the only way to heaven is through Him and asking Him into your heart.

3. It was presented as the greatest sacrifice that anyone has ever made for me.

4. An anointed member gave a sermon and then asked the congregation for a contribution.

5. Just in conversation about my religious background and what church I belonged to, some start quoting Scriptures about being "saved."

6. In church, professionally and not pushy; TV—pushy and almost a joke.

7. It was slightly radical and the presenter seemed close-minded.

8. In a serious manner, usually with someone yelling.

9. Sometimes in a "hellfire and brimstone" version and others quite softly.

10. In all sorts of ways: serious, humorous, blasphemous (some TV evangelists).

11. Positively and convincingly; usually with a great sense that the narrator was sincere and speaking from his heart.

12. Mostly pedantic advice, which assumes I know nothing.

13. On campus—someone was saying the only way to salvation is through Jesus Christ because no one else died for us.

14. By preaching the goodness of Christians and by giving reasons for that goodness; moral superiority.

15. By a fat guy.

16. With vehemence.

17. By a preacher who got so worked up on screen (in front of a huge congregation) he started crying hysterically.

18. As if it were the absolute truth for all.

19. I felt more like it was an advertisement for God than a spiritually uplifting/fulfilling message.

20. TV—preached of humbleness and of man's sins in a luxurious alter [sic].

Survey Question 17

Honestly, how did you react to this presentation?

1. Sad/repulsed—it sends the wrong message to people who do not know better than to look into it.

2. After a while they are all the same and you become numb to the whole thought.

3. It made me think about a lot and I said that I was going to change, but in the end I didn't.

4. Every time I hear the gospel, it brings conviction because I am not doing everything I can for God.

5. I cried, I just can't believe that I am loved that much for a human man to endure that for me. I am nobody and He died for me.

6.   Some experiences were good, others were bad. Some people harass others about it. Sometimes I welcome it and other times I just don't want to hear it.

7.   It makes me realize that I need to make a choice, soon, because I will not live forever. Get my life together!!

8.   It was flashily done. It sickens me. Religion should not be brought to you; you should seek out religion.

9.   I listen because I know they're trying to help because it's important to them, but I forget what they say—just smile and nod.

10. I've just heard it too much. Leave me alone. Well, I take that back… I enjoy a laugh at the wigged chick on TBN.

11. I did not want to listen because I was afraid to fall prey to the emotional presentation used to lure followers.

12. Now I react by trying to get away from it, no matter the presentation style.

13. My reactions vary—sometimes boredom, sometimes fear, sometimes sadness, and many times anger.

14. Some presentations, I learn something new, but most of the presentations are on things I've heard, only done differently. Others create painful realizations and flashbacks.

15. I was wary and was kind of nervous when asked about my personal thoughts or if I wanted to accept Christ into my heart right then and there.

16. The first time I was very resistant and apathetic; gradually I became more open to it.

17. There's times when I have been touched and it really helped me but other times when I shook my head at the superficiality.

18. The truth broke my heart and I could only receive God's love into my life.

19. I'm usually more cynical to the medium of TV. I prefer the spoken message and especially radio because it is non-threatening.

20. I was sure of it, I enjoyed it; but as soon as they start talking about Jesus the Savior, I quickly change stations.

21. I blow if off. I'm a firm believer in Judaism. I respect Christianity but I don't believe or agree. Sure, they tell me I'm wrong, but I don't care.

22. I didn't like it, because it didn't feel like those people truly meant it. It seemed more like a performance.

23. I was moved by people's testimonies.

24. I felt that it was overblown, irrelevant, and morally superfluous.

25. I agree, we are sinners, but I don't see how just by believing we can be cleansed.

26. I am accustomed to hearing it often, so I've grown desensitized to hearing the same basic message repeatedly.

27. I enjoy hearing them and then pointing out the hypocrisy in practice.

28. By rejecting the Bible as the direct Word of God when it was written down by mortals and therefore flawed human beings. The exclusion of others such as non-Christians and gays and the focus on sin and the devil.

29. I thought, "What the f---, this is ridiculous, he needs to get a life; nobody wants to see this."

30. I thought it was a bad idea to present it in a little booklet because people wonder what propaganda you're trying to spread.

31. I honestly said to myself, "This is bull----, who do these preachers think they are?" every time I heard it.

32. Incredulously, I was amazed at how he put down other faiths and the role of women.

Survey Question 18

If you chose to accept the presentation, which factors were most significant in forming the basis of your decision?

1. That someone who does not know me would die for sins and transgressions that I would commit thousands of years later. That is powerful.

2. After a while, they are all the same and you become numb with the whole thought.

3. You can pick out what you agree with; everyone has their own opinion.

4. My preacher, when I was 7 years old, broke it down for me and my family. Life was bad. Jesus was all I needed and He still is. [My pastor] told me the truth about Christianity and I accepted it wholeheartedly.

5. If they (the preacher) could relate the gospel to how we use his advice and word in our daily lives.

6. I found truth in it—and I felt in my heart that I needed God in my life. I knew there was something missing.

7. The presentation started out light and the longer it was, the more deep it got. The message showed me that I was missing Jesus Christ in my life. I need Him. I had a void, and I filled it with Him.

8. My belief in a place called hell.

9. Everything written in the Bible is to be accepted as truth.

10. Realizing that death is certain and God is to be feared.

11. The realization that my life is not my own and that God loves me unconditionally.

12. Based on its accuracy and whether it was trying to force me or invite me; if it tries to invite and allow you to make your own decision I would more likely believe it.

13. Proofs from archeology that show the actual locations of biblical events.

14. The way in which it's presented; is there a forceful attitude? Are you pressured? If so, I hesitate to accept it.

15. I accept and respond well to the positive, tolerant messages because they fit my belief of an all-loving God.

16. It comes down to a choice: to follow personal desires or surrender to Christ. This choice is enabled by Christ, but the decision is ours.

17. The presenter and how honest he seemed in delivering a message that I could understand and use, and wasn't merely trying to change my mind ("not trying to change my mind" meaning convert the person).

18. Personal, real-life anecdotes instead of biblical references that one cannot relate to.

Survey Question 19

If you chose to reject the presentation, which factors were most significant in forming the basis of your decision?

1. The hypocrite people who condemn people to hell.

2. I respond more to presentations that speak to me and [don't] shout or browbeat me. Jesus didn't do these.

3. That money was the major purpose of the presentation or political motives were involved.

4. The extremities of the opinions of the individual. The fact that there was no open-mindedness.

5. Some grown-up yelling and screaming instead of sounding educated and intellectual.

6. TV—laugh and poke fun at the gold chairs they were sitting in. They were just sitting in gold chairs. Jesus didn't have a gold chair.

7. The information given didn't seem desirable or worth my listening time, all because the presenter wanted to shove it down my throat.

8. I reject the idea that Jesus Christ is unique in the fact that He is the embodiment of an omnipotent, omni-benevolent, omniscient God.

9. I believe that man's destiny is a ship steered by the course of environment and ones [sic] own actions. It is not [steered] by some mysterious guy in the sky.

10. The lady's eye make-up smeared because she was so upset and happy about her Lord!

11. The way the person preached love but turned around and preached hate in a sense.

12. Those presentations seem store-bought and fed to those who will swallow it. They always allude to how terrible people are and how we will go to hell if we aren't "saved" and profess our devotion to the Lord.

13. The way it accused other religions of being wrong and heathen-like; oh, and the continuous request for money.

14. The fact that it is fallible, and this has been proven time and time again.

15. Christianity does not = truth. I would reject the presentation because it is preaching Christianity. I am highly educated on the subject and already know that the gospel is not fact.

16. I don't think that the only way to salvation is through Him [Jesus].

17. They are typically white wealthy people giving the presentation and in the audience; I cannot relate when coming from a different socioeconomic background.

18. I read the text and thought the quotes the pastor pulled out as proof of certain beliefs as taken out of context. They didn't seem that way to me when I read the whole passage.

19. It seems to "market" religion too much, whereas I think religion / spirituality should be an individual choice.

20. The preacher discussed how gays were sinners…most of the gays I know are good people who contribute to society, do good deeds, mind their own business.

21. Seemed absurd to some degree, many factors don't entirely add up— think the whole "faith" excuse is bull----.

22. I feel everyone should have their own personal spiritual life and no one should or can preach the "right" way to live or tell me what the Bible is "really" saying.

Survey Question 20

In your opinion, how could the presentation have been improved?

1. It should never be presented as a fairy tale, but as the greatest love story of all times.

2. The gospel should not be used to scare people out of going to hell but to show them the incredible love of Christ and that He died for them and wants to become their life.

3. Some people who present this message need to be more casual about it.

4. Preachers could have been more interesting, but what it boils down to is you. No matter the presentations God can and will call you. You have to answer.

5. While showing people that they are sinful and that sin must be punished is extremely important, you must also let them know that God is love.

6. He could have made me believe him if money wasn't the main topic of his sermon.

7. Be willing to present both sides and then say this is my personal conviction.

8. Less judgmental. I don't know. I don't like or accept the idea that I should feel bad for wanting to have sex, or cuss someone sometimes, or for breathing.

9. Better use of technology to involve younger people.

10. Don't try to save me or convert me or take my money.

11. I think trying to scare people into Christianity, or giving them a guilt trip, is pretty lame. But not all of them did that.

12. Stop shoving religion down my throat is what I think.

13. More empathy could have been shown toward the "enemy."

14. If the preacher had been more loving. When people are being "bullied" into something, they are more likely to resist.

15. No more hypocrisy; don't talk about the compassion and understanding of God and then say its conditional upon your faith or sexuality.

16. Just keep it biblical and professional; no emotion needed!

17. Be less like they're trying to sell you something.

18. I would ask the presenter: Why do I need Christ? Don't tell me I do. We all have the same God, so why should this preaching matter!

19. Stop using the Bible as reference.

20. Could have been much more open-minded and accept other religions as valuable.

21. I have no idea. The Bible is kind of a contradictory text. How about changing that?

22. Don't force-feed abstract lies, as if Christianity is not a tool used to judge and justify anger and violence labeling non-Christians as heathens and having to "save" us.

23. I think if it weren't so overwhelming in terms of instilling fear.

24. More awareness of the skeptical reception.

25. Tone it down; more of speaking directly to people than "selling" a belief that is "right."

Survey Question 21

Did this presentation change your opinion of Christianity in any way?

1. I am firm in my faith, Christianity is just a title; God is the basis for my faith and my belief.

2. Some presentations did. With some I felt insulted.

3. I lost respect, not all, but some, for this religion.

4. Actually, it made me research the new thoughts and made me realize that what I believed was still right.

5. No, there are still crazy people in the world no matter what faith they are. They believe they are right.

6. Yea [sic], I finally believed it.

7. It made me think of being more positive about life.

8. It strengthened my beliefs of absurdity.

9. Sometimes it opens my eyes and changes the way I look at things.

10. This one particular presentation did not change my opinion, rather it influenced me to reflect on my life and relationship w/ God.

11. It makes me reaffirm my belief.

12. Almost makes me ashamed to call myself Christian.

13. The good and bad sermons make me realize Christianity is heavily influenced by its individual members' attitudes, and the messages vary greatly depending upon the attitude of the person delivering it.

14. It reinforced why I am not a Christian.

15. Yes, I felt it was more like they had an agenda.

16. It actually scared me off.

17. Yes, some aggressive and confrontational presentations put a negative view on Christianity.

18. I'm just more and more tired of it.

19. No, in every religion there are nice, moderate people and nut—it just so happens the nuts are on TV, I guess.

20. Yes, because it's not that effective. I wonder why they don't do anything to change it so that more people learn. Isn't that what they want?

Question 23

Briefly state the "gospel" (Christian message) the way you understand it to be.

1. I wish I knew. I have been trying to put everything together. It is embarrassing to me that I do not know. I want to learn more. I believe in God. I just don't really know why or how.

2. Three words: Just be good.

3. I really can't answer this question because I have heard it so many times that I would not know where to start.

4. God said, "Let there be light."

5. Jesus Christ was sent to earth in human form. He lived and taught, showing love, compassion, and humility every moment. He broke away from traditions and set an example of servitude and true love. He was betrayed by one of the disciples (and all humanity) and crucified in a terrible death. Three days later, He rose from the grave and still lives today in my heart. Simply put, "He came to seek and save that which was lost." Jesus loves you so much!

6. Jesus Christ, the Son of God, was born of a virgin. He was completely man, yet completely deity. He came to die for our sins, to pay the price for us so that we could have forgiveness in God's eyes and go to heaven. All men are sinners, and Jesus' sacrifice, which cleansed us of our sins, allows us fellowship with God. We must accept this gift of salvation though, repenting of our sins, and follow Christ. By doing these things, we can spend eternity in heaven.

7. The gospel is sort of a fable that tells of things from sacrifice, love, hate, anger, and of trials people have faced. I understand it and believe it to be a reminder that though we struggle from time to time, we should be thankful and humble to be ALIVE.

8. God created us to know Him. He is holy and perfect. When sin entered the world, there became a gap between mankind and God— because His holiness was too awesome to be in the presence of our sin. Man and God were separated. God chose to come down to earth as a human (Jesus) and take on the punishment of our sins so that the gap could be bridged and we could know Him. If you believe in God and that He sent Jesus to die for your sins and that He arose three days later, you will be saved. Salvation has nothing to do with being good enough or doing good deeds. It is by faith in God alone. God loves us and wants us just as we are. When we gain our salvation we can begin to know God and be transformed from our old self, to a new person. And through that transformation, God can use us to love others and show them His love.

9. Romans 3:23 says we have all sinned and fallen short of God's expectations of us. Only one man, Jesus, who is God's Son, lived a sinless life but He came to die so that we might be able to have a personal relationship with Him. [In] John 14:6 Jesus said, "I am the way, the truth, and the life. No man comes to the Father except through me." In order to have a relationship with God we must believe that Jesus is God's son and accept Him as our personal Lord and Savior. We must admit that we are sinners and believe that Jesus died for our sins on the cross. We must also repent, turn away from our sins and ask for forgiveness. If we truly do this with our heart, then Jesus has changed us. We have been born again and now have a personal relationship with God that will last for eternity!

10. I do not know anything about the gospel.

11. Be respectful to everything and everyone (unless it's different) and have faith.

12. I have no idea.

13. It is trying to convince people that they should be the way you want them to be and not the way they want to be. It is cramming opinions down people's throats.

14. Follow me and I'll tell you what to do and it'll be all right.

15. Love your neighbor as yourself and give the church money.

16. Love thy neighbor more than oneself and above all, love God and His Son, Jesus. If you do you can go to heaven. If you don't follow these and several other rules, you go to hell (this sounds like nonsense).

17. What I like to boil it down to is the so-called Golden Rule, "Do unto others. ... ", and be Christ-like. Now what is the message that we often see? That's why when people tell me that they are a Christian, I often run.

18. I really do not know much about it, but what I do know is that we are all God's children and we should all get along no matter your religion or anything.

19. Jesus Christ died for our sins. For that, we must worship Him. We must pray our sins be forgiven, although technically they already have been. We must also live by a book that hasn't been updated or revised in quite some time. A book one might consider hear-say. Basically, worship Jesus and give us money or you're going to hell.

20. Jesus Christ is the Son of God who was sent to earth to die for our sins. He rose again and is preparing a place with Him in Heaven for all who receive Him.

21. The gospel is that humans are inherently sinful. Nothing we can ever do will make us righteous in the eyes of God. Therefore, a perfect human that is outside the normal set of humans is needed to bridge the gap between the human world and God. That bridge is Jesus Christ, and it

serves as the only connection between humans and God.

22. My cynical self wants to say that the Christian message means "believe in Christ or go to hell," but I know there are good tenants [sic] to live by through the religion but one must sometimes weed through the useless stuff to get to it.

23. All who ask forgiveness for their sins will be given entrance to the kingdom of heaven; the meek shall inherit the earth; turn the other cheek, yadda, yadda, yadda, and then kill Muslims and anyone else whose land you want for your own.

24. The gospel is a guide, not a set path. We must all find our own way down our own path to the same end: deliverance from evil.

25. Act how you think you would be best in this world; be open to everyone and everything, love everyone if possible; make sacrifices for the good of all.

26. Golden Rule—treat others the way you want to be treated. Seek peace over war; forgive others. Have faith in a force for which there is no proof, and you will go to heaven. The life after death is more important than life on earth.

27. You will burn in hell if you don't think the same way we do.

28. Jesus Christ died for our sins and one should believe, repent and be baptized in order to be saved. None of that "praying Jesus into your heart" crap—that is so out of context. The Scripture they use for that is out of Revelation for people that are already baptized.

29. Love those who conform.

30. Jesus suffered and died on the cross for our sins…or something like that. Love your neighbor…do unto others… etc…. We need to live for Him…. etc. The message sounds nice, but the reality also is that Christianity discriminates against homosexuals, women, Jews, Muslims, etc.

31. Distorted lies of a brilliant magician!

32. The gospel is that we must do good and if we don't, we are punished.

33. I think any faith is good if it gives people comfort with themselves and in their life. I do not condone any form of extremism with any religion. I am not a religious person so [the] gospel means nothing to me.

34. It is difficult to know, since the teachings have been so badly mistranslated and then misinterpreted, and parts of it left out of the Bible.

35. Follow this or suffer; follow this or you will never be happy; blah, blah, blah, manipulate the masses and win.

36. If we're talking Christian and not Catholicism, I believe that they're [sic] gospel message is to convert everyone to their cult; it's freaky.

37. I understand it to be that everyone should be treated equally, follow the Golden Rule.

References

Allport, G. W. (1954). *The nature of prejudice*. Reading, MA: Addison-Wesley.

Barna, G. (2003). *Think like Jesus: Make the right decision every time*. Brentwood, TN: Integrity.

Cell, E. (1967). *Religion and contemporary western culture: Selected readings*. Nashville: Abingdon Press.

Chambers, Oswald. (1992). *My Utmost for His Highest*. Grand Rapids, MI: Discovery House.

Ellul, J. (1986). *The subversion of Christianity*. Grand Rapids, MI: William B. Eerdmans.

Kraemer, H. (1957). *The communication of the Christian faith*. London: Lutterworth.

Kraemer, H. (1963). *The Christian message in a non-Christian world* (6th ed.). Grand Rapids, MI: Kregel.

La Violette, F., & Silvert, K. H. (1951). A theory of stereotypes. *Social Forces, 29*, 257-262.

Lewis, R.L., & Lewis, G. (1989). *Learning to preach Like Jesus*. Westchester: Crossway Books.

McKeehan, T., & Joseph, D. (1995). What if I stumble [excerpt spoken by B. Manning]. *On Jesus Freak* [CD]. Franklin, TN: Forefront.

Merton, T. (1955). *No Man Is An Island.* New York: Harcourt, Brace and Company.

Nisbett, R., & Ross, L. (1980). *Human inference: Strategies and shortcomings of social judgment.* Englewood Cliffs, NJ: Prentice Hall.

Noll, M. A. (1995). The scandal of the evangelical mind. Grand Rapids, MI: William B. Eerdmans.

Offner, Hazel (1981). *Moses: A man changed by God.* Downers Grove, Illinois: InterVarsity Press.

Oskamp, S. (1991). *Attitudes and opinions* (2nd ed.). Englewood Clifs, NJ, Prentice-Hall.

Saenger, G. (1953). *The social psychology of prejudice.* New York: Harper & Row.

Tajfel, H. (1981). *Human groups and social categories: Studies in social psychology.* Cambridge: Cambridge University Press.

Tolstoy, Leo (1900). *Pamphlets.* Free Age Press, Maldon, Essex.

The Bible. (1973). New International Version. Grand Rapids, MI: Zondervan.

Willard, Dallas (1990). *The Spirit of the Disciplines: Understanding How God Changes Lives.* San Francisco: Harper Collins.

WEB SOURCES

Chapter One

My husband and I stopped attending church ...
http://answers.yahoo.com/question/index?qid=20061012170615AA95cTE

Chapter Two

I was an all-out supporter of church ...
http://www.experienceproject.com/stories/Love-God-And-Dont-Go-To-Church/242940

One thing we are thankful for is the education ...
http://www.christianchronicle.org/article2158625~From_Tennessee_to_South_Africa,_Christians_give_thanks

Chapter Three

My whole life I had to live with a mask on ...
http://www.heinvites.org/story.php3/0655.html

I had been taught a lie-in church ...
http://www.heinvites.org/story.php3/0327.html

I was like Saul of Tarsus-the chief of the Pharisees ...
http://www.heinvites.org/story.php3/0177.html

Chapter Four

Today, I'm in love with JESUS. All my life ...
http://www.heinvites.org/fullStory.php3/0552.html

I was raised in a church, and everyone thought that I was a Christian ...
http://www.heinvites.org/fullStory.php3/0382.html

Chapter Five

I grew up in a Christian home ...
http://www.heinvites.org/fullStory.php3/0471.html

I want to talk about the Christian stereotype ...
http://ajwood.com/2008/06/11/christian-stereotypes/

It's hard not to stereotype, isn't it? ...
http://ajwood.com/2008/06/11/christian-stereotypes/

I tried Christianity because it seemed like the good thing to do ...
http://www.exchristian.org/

I had an abortion at age nineteen and I was supposed to be a Christian ...
http://www.heinvites.org/story.php3/0489.html

Chapter Six

I felt like I was the lowest, dirtiest thing on earth ...
http://www.heinvites.org/story.php3/0261.html

I will be the first to admit that I am far from perfect ...
http://ajwood.com/2008/06/11/christian-stereotypes/

I know there is some sort of God ...
http://www.exchristian.org/

Adrian Rogers: Don't let counterfeit Christians keep you out of heaven ...
http://www.lwf.org/site/News2?abbr=for_&page=NewsArticle&id=9757&se
curity=1082&news_iv_ctrl=1183

I was sexually abused from age three ...
http://www.heinvites.org/story.php3/0462.html

Chapter Seven

I've learned that there are always a lot of reasons not to do something ...
http://doableevangelism.com/2009/10/05/taking-risks/

Chapter Eight

I'm comfortable in my "missionary skin" because I know ...
by April Terry (personal blog http://faithwarming.blogspot.com)
http://doableevangelism.com/2009/09/28/missionary-me/

The world system encourages you to be your best ...
http://www.christian-faith.com/forjesus/pride-vs-humility

I understand the meaning of loneliness ...
http://www.heinvites.org/story.php3/0302.html

Chapter Nine

After years in radical feminism, Wicca, Hare Krishna ...
http://www.heinvites.org/story.php3/0090.html

John Stott: The great tragedy in the church today ...
http://findarticles.com/p/articles/mi_7042/is_6_126/ai_n28817972/

I was raised by my Christian parents in the church ...
http://www.exchristian.org/

Chapter Ten

I love God more than anything. Years ago I stopped going to church ...
http://www.experienceproject.com/groups/Love-God-But-Dont-Go-To-Church/116053

Unfortunately, I'm at a place in my life where I'm not living it as I feel I should ...
http://www.experienceproject.com/stories/Love-God-But-Dont-Go-To-Church/716768

Sonia's Poem ... "Look up, my child, why do you cry? ...
http://www.heinvites.org/story.php3/0178.html

I grew up seriously confused about my sexuality ...
http://www.heinvites.org/fullStory.php3/0340.html

Chapter Eleven

Christians worldwide report that they are, in effect, too busy for God ...

"Obstacles to Growth" survey conducted by Dr. Michael Zigarelli, associate professor of Management, Charleston Southern University School of Business. As reported by:
http://www.christianpost.com/article/20070730/survey-christians-worldwide-too-busy-for-god/index.html. Further information about the survey can be found at http://assess-yourself.org.

For the past fifteen years, I've been a worker in the church ...
http://www.heinvites.org/story.php3/0423.html

I'm a normal teenager ...
http://www.heinvites.org/fullStory.php3/0380.html

Today was over 100 degrees out ...
http://doableevangelism.com/category/oa-stories/page/2/

Chapter Twelve

I've been praying, and God is changing my "tight-wadness" ...
http://doableevangelism.com/2009/10/15/tightwad/

The reality is that in this life, we never arrive, but in the next ...
http://doableevangelism.com/2006/09/16/193/

Chapter Thirteen

Sometimes folks have asked me about my faith in God ...
http://www.blog4change.org/articles/688/1/This-is-grabbing-life-at-its-deepest-level/Page1.html

I am frequently amazed at the power of listening ...
http://doableevangelism.com/2005/07/17/listening/

I'm going to kill myself, I thought ...
http://www.heinvites.org/fullStory.php3/0480.html

Shannon, a 20-something, is naturally shy and introverted ...
http://doableevangelism.com/category/oa-stories/page/2/

There is a rising tide of confused discontent in our local churches ...
http://overchurched.wordpress.com/about/

I was in line at a grocery store checkout and the lady in front of me ...
http://doableevangelism.com/2009/10/07/telling-on-the-cashier/

Having been in my community for only nine months ...
http://www.heinvites.org/fullStory.php3/0263.html

Chapter Fourteen

I always wanted a father ...

http://www.heinvites.org/story.php3/0364.html

I was 21, unmarried, pregnant, and into drugs and alcohol ...

http://www.heinvites.org/story.php3/0327.html

My testimony is not amazing ...

http://www.heinvites.org/story.php3/0180.html

About the Author

Dr. John Stiles is an author and speaker based in North Carolina, USA. He earned his Ph.D. in Communication and Culture at the University of Southern Mississippi. Formerly Dean and Professor of Communication at Hannam University (HNU) in South Korea, Dr. Stiles now serves as US Director of HNU's Center for International Relations.

An authority in the field of Cross-Cultural Communication, Dr. Stiles has traveled to over seventy countries and all seven continents. He is in demand internationally for his innovative seminar, *Intercultural SuperHighway*. He challenges his audiences to step outside their individual comfort zones and overcome barriers by genuinely relating with others. Throughout a lifetime of venturing into uncharted territory and building cultural bridges, Dr. Stiles has arrived at a definitive conclusion: "To know culture is to know people."

Dr. Stiles is a graduate of Montreat College in North Carolina and Gordon-Conwell Theological Seminary in Massachusetts. He also shares his passion for reaching out to others as the founder of Cutting Edge International Ministries, Inc.

In addition to his writing and speaking, Dr. Stiles thrives on experiential travel involving the pursuit of deep relational culture within the lives of the individuals he meets. He enjoys comedic films, diverse music, and ballroom dancing. A former college basketball player, he is an avid sports fan and participant.

Dr. Stiles is available for speaking engagements and interactive seminars based on this book. Please visit his website for more information or to schedule a presentation for your group. www.allthedamnchristians.com

CPSIA information can be obtained at www.ICGtesting.com
Printed in the USA
BVOW03s1126240114

342884BV00005B/16/P

9 780982 577394